WHY CICERO MATTERS

WHY PHILOSOPHY MATTERS

Series editor: Professor Constantine Sandis,
University of Hertfordshire, UK

Why Philosophy Matters focuses on why a particular philosopher, school of thought, or area of philosophical study really matters. Each book will offer a brief overview of the subject before exploring its reception both within and outside the academy and our authors will also defend different provocative outlooks on where the value of philosophy lies (or doesn't, as the case may be). Why Philosophy Matters is accompanied by an ongoing series of free events (talks, debates, workshops) in Bloomsbury. Podcasts of these events will be freely available on the series page.

Books in this series

Why Iris Murdoch Matters, Gary Browning
Why Medieval Philosophy Matters, Stephen Boulter
Why Solipsism Matters, Sami Pihlström
Why Climate Breakdown Matters, Rupert Read
Why Delusions Matter, Lisa Bortolotti

Also available from Bloomsbury

Epictetus's 'Encheiridion', Scott Aikin and William O. Stephens
Nietzsche's Renewal of Ancient Ethics, Neil Durrant

WHY CICERO MATTERS

VITTORIO BUFACCHI

BLOOMSBURY ACADEMIC
LONDON • NEW YORK • OXFORD • NEW DELHI • SYDNEY

BLOOMSBURY ACADEMIC
Bloomsbury Publishing Plc
50 Bedford Square, London, WC1B 3DP, UK
1385 Broadway, New York, NY 10018, USA
29 Earlsfort Terrace, Dublin 2, Ireland

BLOOMSBURY, BLOOMSBURY ACADEMIC and
the Diana logo are trademarks of Bloomsbury Publishing Plc

First published in Great Britain 2023
Reprinted in 2023

Copyright © Vittorio Bufacchi, 2023

A catalogue record for this book is available from the British Library.

A catalog record for this book is available from the Library of Congress.

ISBN: HB: 978-1-3503-7667-0
        PB: 978-1-3503-7668-7
        ePDF: 978-1-3503-7669-4
        eBook: 978-1-3503-7670-0

Series: Why Philosophy Matters

Typeset by Integra Software Services Pvt. Ltd.
Printed and bound in Great Britain

To find out more about our authors and books visit www.bloomsbury.com
and sign up for our newsletters.

For Alex Davis
who once lent me a book on Cicero
that I never returned

Contents

Preface

This book is about the greatest chickpea in the history of humanity, Roman philosopher and statesman Marcus Tullius, better known as Cicero. 'Cicero' was not his last name, but his nickname, or to be precise his *cognomen*. It was common in Ancient Rome to be referred to by a nickname, which would then pass down through the generations. Some were fortunate to have Magnus ('The Great') as their nickname. In Cicero's case it was different, for it comes from the Latin word *cicer*, meaning 'chickpea'. This was a reference to the shape of his nose, as Plutarch (46 to post-119 AD) explains, 'a slight nick in the end of his nose like the cleft of a chickpea'. That's how Marcus Tullius became known as Cicero, also Rome's greatest orator, philosopher, lawyer and (possibly) statesman.

The imperial historian Titus Livius, generally known as Livy, writing only a few decades after Cicero's death, quipped that one would need a Cicero to sing his praises. Sadly, today Cicero does not get much attention, except from Ancient Roman history buffs and wayward political philosophers like me. And anyway, Cicero certainly does not get the admiration he deserves. This book is an attempt to bring Cicero to the attention of a broader public, especially those with an interest in philosophy and politics.

Cicero was a complex person: insecurity blended with bravado, hesitancy with courage, unscrupulous deeds with highly principled action. A unique combination held together by a wicked sense of humour, often spectacularly insensitive. It was a bad joke, at the wrong time, about the wrong person, that ultimately cost him his life. We could think of Cicero as the amalgamation of a powerful trinity: Plato (the philosopher), Obama (the politician) and Woody Allen (the comedian). Like Plato, Cicero used philosophy to guide his political practice. Like Obama, Cicero came from humble roots and defied political odds to become the most powerful elected politician in Rome at the time. And not unlike Woody Allen, apart from the jokes, at the age of sixty Cicero married a woman much younger than him. But more about that later.

I wrote the book thinking of my children, Jacobo and Natalie. They are the next generation. Cicero famously said: 'While there's life, there's hope.' My generation has gone a long way towards extinguishing life from our planet, so Cicero may have been too optimistic. Politics, as always, is at the root of the problem. We can only hope it is not too late to pull back from the brink. In the arduous task ahead of us needed to get us out of the present political quagmire, Cicero could prove to be a valiant guide.

Speaking of my children, for the last few years Natalie and Jacobo have had to live with an extra member of our family: Marcus Tullius. They rolled their eyes whenever I mentioned Cicero, as I often did, and perhaps rightly so. They have been spectacularly resilient (I'm tempted to say 'stoic') and supportive of their absent-minded father who remembers the minutiae of Catiline's trial in 63 BC but forgets about rowing training or swimming lessons. My feeling towards them is not dissimilar to Cicero's feelings for his daughter Tullia, who he loved more than life itself. When Tullia died during childbirth, life for Cicero lost meaning, and he gradually lost the will to live.

I'm very grateful to Giorgia Anile, James Brohan, Ellen Byrne, Lucy Camille-Victoire Dubert and Ciarán Lynch for reading the entire manuscript and offering me very valuable feedback: *gratias tibi ago*. My gratitude to my editor at Bloomsbury, Colleen Coalter, for her encouragement and support over the past few years. And my sincere thanks also to three anonymous reviewers at Bloomsbury who were meticulous but constructive, scrupulous but positive. No author could ask for more.

My Latin teacher Áine Cregan made a valiant effort to teach me Latin. I'm very grateful to her for all the industry and labour she put into it, and for making Latin fun. It is not her fault if I can't remember the fourth Latin conjugation for the gerund. *Mea culpa*. It is one of my great regrets that I didn't study Latin in school, and I wish more schools today offered Latin as an option.

My thanks also to my brother Roberto 'Doom' Bufacchi, with whom I explored many ruins, museums and exhibitions on Ancient Rome over a period of many years. I hope we will resume our cultural and architectural adventures soon.

During the long process of writing this book I have been fortunate to teach an undergraduate course on Cicero at University College Cork (Ireland) to students of philosophy, politics and classics. I'm very grateful to all my students whose enthusiasm convinced me that Cicero deserved a bigger audience. It was a lot of fun (for me) trying to explain to them the brilliance of Cicero, and why Cicero could change their lives. The lectures I delivered for this course form the backbone of this book. I'm also duty-bound to report that I have learned as much from my students as they have learned from me, if not more.

My friend Alex Davis, to whom this book is dedicated, is almost single-handedly responsible for the existence of the book you are about to read. One evening over dinner he made the grave mistake of lending me a copy of Robert Harris's *Imperium*, the first book in the outstanding historical fiction trilogy on Cicero's life. This act of generosity sparked my interest in Cicero's life, but also his philosophy. Needless to say, I never returned the book, an act that Cicero would not approve of – although he would no doubt approve of the fact that people are still writing books on him more than 2,000 years after his death. Thank you, Alex. I must also express my sincere gratitude to Robert Harris for having rekindled the interest on Cicero for me and for millions of other readers across the world.

My wife Jools is the most important person in my life, and like our children she also had to put up with a lot of 'Jools, listen to this! Cicero once said …', probably more than anyone should, notwithstanding wedding vows. Nevertheless, one last time, Jools, listen to this! Cicero said: 'Love is the attempt to form a friendship inspired by beauty.' I couldn't have said it better myself.

Cork, August 2022

Introduction: It's all Shakespeare's fault

While there's life, there's hope

MARCUS TULLIUS CICERO (*LETTERS TO ATTICUS*)

A student walks into a bookshop, looking for something to read on the most famous philosopher, orator and statesman of Ancient Rome: Marcus Tullius Cicero (106–43 BC). She is slightly puzzled, and more-than-slightly disappointed. On the 'Ancient History' bookshelf all the usual suspects are there, from Mary Beard to H. H. Scullard, Tom Holland and Klaus Bringmann, and almost inevitably the much older text by R. H. Barrow *The Romans*, but this student is looking for a book entirely devoted to Cicero.

On the shelves there are biographies of various illustrious figures from Ancient Rome. Rather predictably, there are more books on Julius Caesar than about anyone else, but not a single book on Marcus Tullius Cicero. Unperturbed, she goes to another, bigger bookshop. Here she finds even more books on Julius Caesar, but only one book on Cicero, by Gesine Manuwald, published in 2015. Manuwald's book *Cicero* is superb, erudite and witty in equal measures, a must read for anyone interested in how this 'new man' from the small town of Arpinium 120 kilometres from Rome changed the course of Roman history. She buys Manuwald's book, but wonders why there is so little written on Cicero, and so much published on Julius Caesar. Why does Julius Caesar always get all the attention, while Cicero is almost universally neglected? And what does this say about modern politics and political culture?

In the public imagination, which in this case can conveniently be quantified in the number of books devoted to an historical grandee, Julius Caesar towers over Cicero. Julius Caesar gets a disproportionate attention not only by authors keen to meet the unquenchable curiosity of readers fascinated by this dictator[1] but also by marketing gurus, considering that Caesar also pops up on covers of books not about himself but more generally on Ancient Rome; Caesar is the undisputed, heavy-weight, universally recognized face of that era.[2]

The popularity and admiration for Julius Caesar defies time and logic. He has, and always has had, a cult following, notwithstanding his monarchical and dictatorial tendencies. Or perhaps because of it.[3] Much has been made of Julius Caesar's legendary clemency, or merciful nature, whereby he spared the lives of his enemies, but he also had a blood-thirsty streak, which he enforced with ruthless efficiency. Of his campaign in Gaul, modern-day France and Germany, it has been said that requisitions of food and punitive devastations completed a human, economic and ecological disaster probably unequalled until the conquest of the Americas.[4]

In 51 BC, after the Siege of Uxellodunum, Julius Caesar decided against executing the Gallic survivors, instead he had the hands of all the men of military age cut off. In another incident in 57 BC, also when serving as a general of Roman legions in Gaul, after defeating the Germanic Atuatuci tribe, Julius Caesar records selling 53,000 slaves in one day, for his private profit. It would not be hyperbolic or whimsical to describe Julius Caesar's conquest of Gaul as an act of genocide. In fact, although Romans were accustomed to levels of violence well beyond our imagination, even his contemporaries criticized Julius Caesar for the unnecessary, vicious and brutal violence that accompanied his legions throughout Europe.[5] In one famous incident, chronicled in detail by Julius Caesar himself in Book IV of *De Bello Gallico* (The Battle for Gaul), a battle took place in 55 BC resulting in the genocide of between 150,000 and 200,000 Germanic tribespeople, including women and children. Julius Caesar reported how he exterminated virtually an entire population with an eerie sense of pride and swagger:

> I sent the cavalry to hunt them down. When the Germans heard cries behind them and saw that their own people were being killed, they threw their weapons, abandoned their standards, and rushed out of the camp. When they reached the confluence of the Moselle and the Rhine, they saw they had no hope of escaping farther. A large number of them were killed and the rest flung themselves into the river, where they perished overcome by panic, exhaustion, and the force of the current.[6]

Today we would not dream of admiring a modern dictator guilty of genocide, and yet we seem to make an exception for Julius Caesar, who to this day remains the emblem of one of history's greatest (and blood-stained) empires, and still a role model for many politicians.[7]

Julius Caesar's assassination on the ides of March in 44 BC turned him into a martyr, a victim of injustice, and since then people have been wondering how history would have unfolded had it not been deprived of one of its most brilliant and charismatic figures.

Julius Caesar was a violent despot, a ruthless autocrat, while Cicero stood up for the rule of law, the politics of compromise and for constitutional practice. And yet, compared to Caesar and Augustus (Octavian), Cicero today is still relatively unknown, an historical figure generally misunderstood and universally unappreciated outside of those universities that are not closing their departments of classics.

As to the reasons for the global fascination for Julius Caesar, and the equally comprehensive indifference towards Cicero, pop psychology could be summoned to speculate on the near-universal appeal of the gory in human nature, and to the allure of glory. The popularity of the fantasy drama television series *Game of Thrones*, a perfect example of how to make gratuitous violence and sex scenes profitable, taps into the same trait of human psychology as the admiration for Julius Caesar. It is best however not to indulge in asinine speculations. Instead, I want to suggest a different, counter-intuitive, perhaps uncanny explanation: the Bard has much to answer for.

Shakespeare

Shakespeare wrote an entire play on Julius Caesar. He also wrote another play, *Antony and Cleopatra*, and of course Marc Antony was another sworn enemy of Cicero. But Shakespeare never wrote a play on Cicero. *Julius Caesar* is one of Shakespeare's best loved and most influential plays. In Act 3, Scene 2, Marc Antony makes a speech, at the funeral of Julius Caesar, that to this day remains one of the most memorable soliloquys ever written by the world's favourite playwright; an oration that contains some of the most haunting opening lines ever written in a play, before or since:

Friends, Romans, countrymen, lend me your ears;
I come to bury Caesar, not to praise him;
The evil that men do lives after them,
The good is oft interred with their bones,
So let it be with Caesar ... The noble Brutus
Hath told you Caesar was ambitious:
If it were so, it was a grievous fault,
And grievously hath Caesar answered it ...
Here, under leave of Brutus and the rest,
(For Brutus is an honourable man;
So are they all; all honourable men)
Come I to speak in Caesar's funeral ...
He was my friend, faithful and just to me:
But Brutus says he was ambitious;
And Brutus is an honourable man ....
He hath brought many captives home to Rome,
Whose ransoms did the general coffers fill:
Did this in Caesar seem ambitious?
When that the poor have cried, Caesar hath wept:
Ambition should be made of sterner stuff:
Yet Brutus says he was ambitious;
And Brutus is an honourable man.
You all did see that on the Lupercal
I thrice presented him a kingly crown,

Which he did thrice refuse: was this ambition?

Yet Brutus says he was ambitious;

And, sure, he is an honourable man.

I speak not to disprove what Brutus spoke,

But here I am to speak what I do know.

You all did love him once, not without cause:

What cause withholds you then to mourn for him?

O judgement! thou art fled to brutish beasts,

And men have lost their reason .... Bear with me;

My heart is in the coffin there with Caesar,

And I must pause till it come back to me.

Flawlessly crafted, this speech is delivered by Marc Antony, a man who, from what we know of him, had many vices, for example his legendary, excessive drinking. It is believed that he even wrote a treatise on drunkenness, which may be one of the charred scrolls recently discovered in Herculaneum, near Pompeii.[8] Admittedly, Marc Antony also had some positive attributes, primarily as a military general, but eloquence was not one of them. And yet Shakespeare puts rousing, evocative, poetic words in his mouth, to the benefit of both Marc Antony and Julius Caesar. And Cicero? Shakespeare chooses to make Cicero appear like a minor historical figure, being conspicuous by his absence in this play: he only gets a few lines, of no significance, and worst still he is even the butt of Shakespeare's jokes. In one passage in Shakespeare's *Julius Caesar*, Cassius asks Casca how Cicero responded to Julius Caesar's mock coronation, and Casca says 'he spoke Greek'. For reasons that will never be known, Shakespeare depicts Cicero as either an irrelevant intellectual, or a coward. Or perhaps both.[9]

To blame Shakespeare for Julius Caesar's prominence in our collective public imagination, and also for Cicero's related obscurity, is possibly churlish, and probably unfair on Shakespeare. After all, Dante Alighieri also carries some of the blame. In his *Divine Comedy*, in the deepest circle of the Inferno, where the worst sinners are flung, we find three historical characters whose punishment for their sins is to be eternally chewed by Satan's three mouths. One of them is Judas Iscariot, who famously betrayed Jesus. The other two are Gaius Cassius Longinus, the most senior of Julius Caesar's assassins, and Marcus Brutus, who betrayed and conspired in Julius Caesar's murder. In Dante's Inferno wrongdoing against Julius Caesar outnumber misdeed against Jesus Christ by two to one, which makes one wonder whether for Dante the murder of Julius Caesar constituted a more serious crime against humanity than the betrayal and execution of Jesus Christ.

This well-documented disparity between the allure of Julius Caesar compared to Cicero may seem like a trivial issue, a mere curiosity, but in fact it is a microcosm of a bigger, and much more serious, political reality. The perpetual popularity of Julius Caesar is also a reflection of the current political climate, dominated by the global resurgence of the far-right, driven by authoritarian populists.

Roman populism

Camila Vergara has described populism as 'plebeian politics', tracing the origins of plebeian populism to Ancient Rome: '[populism today] springs from the politicization of wealth inequality in reaction to systemic corruption and the immiseration of the masses, an attempt to balance the scales of social and political power between the ruling elite and the popular sectors'.[10] She is right; in order to understand the phenomenon of populism today we need to go back in time a few thousand years to Ancient Rome.

Consider the case of Publius Clodius Pulcher, better known simply as Clodius, one of Ancient Rome's best-loved bad boys. He was a social rascal and a political radical, scandalously promiscuous and libertine. Gaining notoriety in 62 BC when he gate-crashed a solemn, all-female religious festival, allegedly to seduce Julius Caesar's second wife Pompeia, he then became one of the most violent and politically dangerous leaders of a populist faction that engineered the exile of Cicero from Rome. Clodius went on to terrorize the streets of Rome with his private militia, just like Mussolini's *squadristi* used violence to intimidate anyone who opposed his fascist party from 1919 onwards.

There is one curious aspect of Clodius's life that makes his political biography compelling, and of particular interest to anyone studying populism today: Clodius was born into a rich, powerful, established, patrician family. What he did in order to gain political power was both unprecedented and remarkable: he turned his back on the patrician roots of his family and asked to be adopted by a plebeian family. As Mary Beard explains: '[Clodius] has gone down in history as the mad patrician who not only arranged to be adopted into a plebeian family in order to stand for the tribunate but also put two fingers up to the whole process by choosing an adoptive father younger than himself.'[11]

In an innovative, non-monarchical political system defined by a complex balancing act between an elite of senators of conservative disposition, dead set on maintaining the status quo with all the privileges it bestowed to the small number of ruling families, and a growing underclass of plebeian citizens who had some political representation through the appointment of official tribunes of the people (*tribuni plebis*), the populist card was often used in the years of the Roman Republic to press on with radical political reforms, often accompanied by bloodbaths.

Before Clodius caused havoc and brought mayhem to Rome, the long shadow of populism was cast by two legendary brothers, Tiberius and Gaius Gracchus. Their political agendas and methods were distinctly populist. One brother attempted to pass land reform legislation that would redistribute the major aristocratic landholdings among the urban poor and veterans, the other brother pushed for a subsidized quantity of grain to each citizen of Rome. Both were assassinated for their political vision.

The Gracchus brothers have been the subject of admiration and loathing in equal measures. Their actions have inspired a millennial dispute, never to be settled, whether they ought to be considered valiant socialist martyrs, or merely political opportunists. It is fair to say that the jury is still out, and that this question will never be resolved: the Gracchus brothers are such stuff as political dreams and myths are made on.[12]

The parallels between the Gracchus brothers and Clodius are many, including the fact that although the Gracchus brothers were officially plebeians, they were born into the old and noble Sempronia family, of pure patrician pedigree. Their father held all the major political offices in the Republic: tribune of the plebs, praetor, consul and censor. Their mother was a patrician, Cornelia Africana, daughter of Scipio Africanus, a hero of the Punic war against Carthage.

The populist card was also played by another influential aspiring politician during Cicero's lifetime: Lucius Sergius Catiline. Born a patrician in 108 BC in one of Rome's oldest and most influential families, Catiline belonged to that segment of Rome's established nobility that simply assumed that their family names were sufficient to secure a role of influence in Rome's political hierarchy. Catiline grew up in the belief that because of his name and family history he had a right to the highest political office, and that winning an election was always going to be a mere formality.

Catiline run for consulship the same year as Cicero, in 62 BC, and he did what everyone else was doing at the time: take out huge debts to bribe the electorate. His gamble did not pay off, and he refused to accept that he could be deprived of his divine right to a consulship by a 'new man' (*novus homo*) like Cicero, someone whose family lacked senatorial ancestors, and who did not bribe his way to the top.

Catiline ran for election the following year, on a populist ticket: he offered free food and drink to the electorate on voting day, and he conveniently and unapologetically campaigned for the cancellation of debt, which would have appealed to many urban plebs at the time. This was known as the economic policy of *tabulae novae* or 'clean slate'. When he lost the election for the second time, he decided the best strategy was to take power by military means, destroying the democratic pretences of the Republic, and establish himself as sole ruler of Rome. This plot for a *coup d'état*, which he orchestrated in the second half of 63 BC, was foiled by Cicero who at the time held the consulship. It has gone down in history as the Catiline Conspiracy, also as Cicero's finest hour.[13] That Cicero's triumph over Catiline went to Cicero's head is a well-documented fact, and he was very proud to be referred to as 'father of the fatherland' (*parentem patriae*) and 'saviour of the Republic', as he frequently reminded everyone around him for the rest of his life.[14] Catiline was killed in battle against the Republican army in January 62 BC.

Where Clodius, the Gracchus brothers and Catiline failed, Julius Caesar succeeded: born into a powerful and privileged family, Julius Caesar's populist appeal was instrumental to undermining the rule of law, culminating in his appointment as 'dictator for life'. As Kathryn Tempest rightly says, 'Caesar represented the kind of populist politician that had long been feared.'[15] Julius Caesar used violence to fuel a revolution that put an end to an old order based on rights, and ushered in a new order founded on might. The Roman Republic, a constitutional system grounded on the rule of law, where moderation was assured through a system of checks and balances not dissimilar to modern constitutional democracies, was replaced by a military dictatorship, with the *Dux* wielding absolute power, backed by the threat of violence.[16] Because of what we know about modern fascism, Julius Caesar's continuing appeal is a worrying phenomenon.[17] At this particular moment in time, the rehabilitation of Cicero as an antidote to the myth of the strong man of history feels urgent, and important; this book is an effort in this endeavour.[18]

Lessons from Ancient Rome

This book was written with the expressed intention to give the fictitious student in our story what she is looking for. I would like to think that there are many non-fictional students, scholars and ordinary decent citizens who will find this book of some interest. Its aim is to stem the tide of the persistent cult of authoritarian populists by counterbalancing the disproportionate number of books on Julius Caesar one finds in bookshops across the world compared to books on Cicero.

It is a familiar cliché to explore current affairs through the lenses of Ancient Rome. Many books, and even more articles, in learned journals and newspapers have been written with this goal in mind. In the UK, until the end of the Second World War all politicians and civil servants were well versed in classics as preparation for their profession, and the history of Ancient Rome featured prominently in their syllabus.[19]

This antiquated approach to contemporary affairs can have its rewards, but there are also pitfalls in this all-to-common exercise in historical juxtaposition. It is not as simple as it seems. Mary Beard, arguably the greatest living historian of Ancient Rome, is fully cognizant of this and rightly warns us that Roman history offers very few direct lessons for us, and no simple list of dos and don'ts. There is no simple Roman model to follow, or reject. She is right, and yet Roman history still matters, and we disregard it at our peril. As Cicero once said, anyone can make mistakes, but only an idiot persists in their error. We can't escape Roman political thought, in part because it provided us with the lexicon of our political language, from power to justice, citizenship to domination, constitutionalism to dictatorship. Ancient Rome is where our ideas about politics come from; as Mary Beard reminds us, whether we like it or not, we have inherited from Rome many of the fundamental principles and symbols with which we define and debate politics and political action.[20]

Although Cicero is the main protagonist of this book, this book is not just about Cicero, and it is not (yet another) book on the history of Ancient Rome. Instead, this book is as much about us, and our democracy in the twenty-first century, as it is about Ancient Rome.

It is not my intention to give readers an historically detailed account of events in first-century BC Rome. There are many superb books on the history of Ancient Rome, therefore readers so inclined are recommended to read Mary Beard's *SPQR*, or Tom Holland's *Rubicon*, or HH Sculland's *From the Gracchi to Nero*.[21] But whatever you do, do not go near Boris Johnson's *The Dream of Rome*.[22] For an historical analysis of the Roman Republic, I recommend Klaus Bringmann's *A History of the Roman Republic*, or David Shotter's *The Fall of the Roman Republic*, or Mary Beard and Michael Crawford's *Rome in the Late Republic*.[23] For those interested in intellectual history, for the period 63 to 43 BC there is simply no better book than Katharina Volk's *The Roman Republic of Letters*.[24] And for those interested in military history, Richard Alston's *Rome's Revolution* is an enjoyable page-turner.[25] There are also a few excellent biographies that take us through Cicero's life, by Anthony Everitt, Kathryn Tempest, Elizabeth Rawson, David Shackleton Bailey.[26] Going back a few years we have the continually charming two-volume *Cicero and his Friends*, by Gaston Boissier, originally published in French in 1865, and *The Life of Cicero*, by Anthony Trollope, from 1880.

I would also strongly recommend the trilogy of historical novels on Cicero's life by Robert Harris, *Imperium*; *Lustrum*; *Dictator*: a perfect example of how to combine fiction with history; any reader who takes history seriously, but has an insatiable appetite for the misconducts and misdemeanours of Ancient Romans, will not be disappointed.

The book you are about to read is different from those listed above: this book is not about understanding Cicero in his historical, intellectual or philosophical context. I'm not trying to reconstruct the motivations of an historical figure who lived 2,000 years ago, as is the case with Thomas Mitchell's *Cicero the Senior Statesman* or Christian Habicht's *Cicero the Politician*.[27] Instead this book is written from the point of view of the twenty-first century, and the predicament we find ourselves in today. This book is for readers who, like me, are concerned about the current state of affairs in global politics, where authoritarian far-right populists are all rallying against the foundations of our democratic practice. What all far-right politicians have in common is a commitment to the political philosophy of Caesarism.

Notwithstanding the many discrepancies between first-century BC Rome and our twenty-first century, and all the pitfalls associated with naïve, simplistic comparisons, there is one resemblance between the world of Cicero and our world today that cannot be overlooked: these are dangerous times, not dissimilar from what Cicero experienced in Rome in his time. In Europe, modern democracy is still only a green shoot, having emerged after the horrors of the Second World War. In the United States democracy has allegedly been around for a little longer, although for the first hundred years or so it coexisted with slavery, which makes one question its sincerity. The Roman Republic lasted for the best part of 500 years, and yet it came to an end with the death of Cicero. Liberal democracy has been around a lot less than the Roman Republic, and being younger it is perhaps also more fragile. Today our modern democracies face their most daunting test in many years. It is impossible to disagree with Larry Diamond when he reminds us that 'there is nothing inevitable about the triumph of democracy'.[28]

Democracies will always have enemies. It would be foolish, and unpardonable, for us to take our hard-fought democracy for granted. Viktor Orbán in Hungary is not a Julius Caesar, and certainly not an Octavian. The only thing that Donald Trump has in common with Pompey the Great (*Pompeius Magnus*) is the quiff. But there are traits in their leadership that carry echoes of a Marius or a Sulla, who were not responsible for bringing down the Roman Republic, although they did enough damage to weaken its foundations, showing the way for others, principally Julius Caesar, to complete their project.

The ultimate goal in writing this book is to suggest a different way to think about political engagement today, and how Cicero can help us realize this new political imaginary. This book is primarily a reflection on where philosophy overlaps with politics, although it wants to be much more than an analysis of an important historical figure in the distant history of Western philosophy. Above all, this book is also about the precarious state of democracy in the twenty-first century, and how a philosopher wearing a toga in Ancient Rome can lend us a hand to reinforce our republic. In the last analysis, this book wants to show that our world today needs a Cicero more than it needs (yet another) Julius Caesar.

In Chapter 1, the focus will be on Cicero's love for philosophy, and what philosophy can contribute to politics, political activism and political participation. In an age when anti-intellectualism is running rampant, Cicero had reassuring words on the indispensable work philosophers make, and why the common good needs philosophy.

Chapter 2 will investigate Cicero's treatise on ethics *On Duties*. Here we find confirmation for the view, unpopular today in some quarters, especially in the corridors of power, that politics cannot be separated from ethics. For Cicero politics is nothing more than the active branch of ethics.

Chapter 3 will analyse the political philosophy of republicanism, and in particular Cicero's highly influential text *On the Republic*, where Cicero presents a philosophical case in defence of a political system for the people, by the people. Here Cicero sets out the virtues of a mixed constitution, arguably the most basic idea at the root of any modern democracy; and yet we have seen how in recent years, in many different parts of the world, including in the United States and Europe, this simple institutional mechanism has come under increasing attack by the executive branch of right-wing governments, hell-bent on curbing the independent power of the judiciary.

The next two chapters will focus on two of Cicero's more introspective philosophical texts: *On Friendship* and *On Old Age*. Contrary to what may seem at first, these texts carry a political message. Friendship (Chapter 4) speaks to our need for social communication and acceptance, the first building block of a relational theory of personal and political identity. Old age (Chapter 5) is an inevitable stage of human existence, if one is lucky enough to get there. Today we live in a world where those in 'old age' are a significant segment of the world population, and since we all live longer than our ancestors, the topic of 'old age' has become even more politically and existentially meaningful.

Chapter 6 will suggest that Cicero can still be a role model for us today. Cicero truly believed that a strong Republic needs deep cultural roots, and he refused to separate the rough and tumble of politicking in the Forum from his other cerebral pursuits. Cicero turned politics into a higher, intellectual form of art. He believed in education, in culture, and above all in the power of philosophy to instil morality. Reading Cicero today is a reminder that culture is, or ought to be, the foundation of any modern democracy, and books its building blocks. However, at the end of this chapter some of Cicero's major shortcomings will be analysed, including the remarkable story of how Cicero's witticism got him killed.

Finally, the Epilogue will propel us to the twenty-first century, to the lessons we need to learn from Cicero to save our modern democracies. It will examine a prevalent phenomenon in global politics today: the rise of authoritarian, corrupt, far-right populism. This is arguably the biggest threat to our democracy today, and something that ought to be taken very seriously. Cicero had to deal with a similar threat more than 2,000 years ago, and it was a wave of authoritarian populism that in the end brought the Roman Republic to its knees. We must not make the same mistake, and there are important lessons we can learn from Cicero on this score. Above all, we must rediscover our obligations, today, as voters and citizens. In a democracy we all have rights, including the right to pursue our self-interest, but we must not forget that we also have duties, to each other and to justice more generally. Cicero's writings on these and many other issues are still pertinent.

1

Cicero, *homo philosophicus*

'In times of war, law falls silent'.
MARCUS TULLIUS CICERO (PRO MILONE)

We live in the age of *Homo Oeconomicus*. The Latin here is misleading, since this concept is not more than 250 years old, and there is no known reference to *Homo Oeconomicus* in the Latin texts of antiquity. But the English translation, 'Economic Man', sounds daft, while *Homo Oeconomicus* gives this concept a lustre of authority and solemnity it otherwise lacks. This explains in part why in advanced capitalist society *Homo Oeconomicus* is venerated as a quasi-celestial article of faith.

When the idea of *Homo Oeconomicus* was first proposed, it was merely to capture one aspect of human behaviour in its crudest form. The simple idea that we are always and only motivated by our self-interest, which is (wrongly) equated to an overwhelming, awe-inspiring desire to maximize our wealth, is not something that even

Adam Smith could take seriously. But what started as a caricature was turned into a pseudo-scientific truth, and today the essence of human nature has become synonymous with this reductionist view of humanity.

Over the course of the last two centuries what started as a rough-and-ready description of human nature morphed into something quite different. We appeal to *Homo Oeconomicus* no longer to explain our behaviour but to justify it. *Homo Oeconomicus* has mutated from a descriptive, crass reduction of one aspect of human nature, to a claim of normative veracity. In our modern society the propensity for material advancement in the form of monetary gain is something universally lauded and widely eulogized, to the detriment of other moral values, including the risk of human extinction via climate change and global warming.

If we are to find a feasible alternative to the destructive trajectory of advanced capitalism, it is necessary to find a viable alternative to *Homo Oeconomicus*. This is where Cicero can come to our rescue. Cicero lived his life according to an ideal which could be referred to as *Homo Philosophicus*, and we must learn to do the same.[1]

Ancient Rome was not a society that acknowledged or rewarded meritocracy. Life in Rome was organized around rigid, hierarchical social classes, with clearly defined gender roles. Whether you were born patrician or plebeian, slave or Roman citizen, man or woman, would determine the course of your life. The political elite in Rome all came from a handful of rich, powerful families that claimed they could trace their roots to the founding of Rome in 753 BC. All the most powerful men in Rome, bar a few exceptions, came from these families. Cicero's family was not one of them. His family was economically secure, but of no particular social standing, and in Rome honour was immensely more important than money.

Cicero was born with two major handicaps: he was not born in Rome, and he did not come from a patrician family. Born in 106 BC in the small hill town of Arpinium (modern-day Arpino, not far from Frosinone) 120 miles south-east of Rome, Cicero fought all his life the prejudice against him for being a 'new man', *novus homo*. Cicero himself perfectly captures the obstacles he faced: 'I have not the same privileges as those men of noble birth on whom all the blessings of the Roman people are showered as they lie asleep.'[2]

A notoriously complex man, driven by a concoction of contrasting feelings and dispositions, a mix of hard work and arrogance, pragmatism and loyalty, helped along by a natural gift for intellectual endeavours, Cicero achieved something that has been unmatched for the last 2,000 years: he is the only philosopher to have held the highest political office. Other contenders for the title of undisputed best philosopher in politics might include Seneca and Marcus Aurelius. Seneca's philosophical work is impressive, but he never held an elected position, even though as political advisor to emperor Nero he had considerable influence. Marcus Aurelius was emperor from 161 to 180 AD and a Stoic philosopher, but his only known philosophical work, the *Meditations*, is lightweight compared to Cicero's much more substantial output. Marcus Aurelius does not engage systematically with any text in the history of philosophy, instead he is happy to dish out his pearls of wisdom devoid of any critical analysis.

In 63 BC, Cicero was elected consul of the Roman Republic, the highest political office at the time, the modern equivalent of being elected Prime Minister or President. But Cicero was more than a successful politician; we also know Cicero for his extensive philosophical output: on rhetoric, on politics, on ethics, on epistemology, on philosophical questions regarding friendship and old age, on just war, on good and evil, facing death and the good life, emotions and our mental state. Unlike Plato and Aristotle, Cicero did not write about logic or the natural sciences, instead his focus tended to be predominantly, although not exclusively, of an ethical nature. In that sense his philosophical output was slightly narrower than the Greek philosophers he greatly admired, even though he would never admit it. In his *Tusculan Disputations*, Book 2, Cicero claims that he does not limit his philosophizing to a few subjects, 'for philosophy is a matter in which it is difficult to acquire a little knowledge without acquainting yourself with many, or all its branches'.[3]

Plato famously speculated about the Philosopher King, in the process drawing suspicion to the philosophical profession and making life for philosophers miserable ever since. The idea that philosophical training is sufficient to justify authoritarianism and despotism is ludicrous, dangerous and a disservice to all philosophers. Perhaps Cicero was right when he said that 'there is nothing so absurd that some philosopher has not already said it',[4] except that Cicero truly believed in the redeeming powers of philosophy, for both the individual and society.

Today intellectuals tend to be looked down upon. Thinkers usually work in Ivory Towers, safe havens where they are not persecuted (at least most of the time)[5] but which also keeps them at a safe distance from centres of influence. A few of them venture out, and are even well-received on television or the radio or on the OpEd pages of a few newspapers: Mary Beard comes to mind in the UK; Jurgen Habermas in Germany; Umberto Eco in Italy; but they are the exception. The rule is that it is extremely rare to find intellectuals, and especially philosophers, walking the corridors of power. Isaac Asimov perfectly captures the antipathy towards people who prioritize knowledge and learning when he said that 'Anti-intellectualism has been a constant thread winding its way through our political and cultural life, nurtured by the false notion that democracy means "my ignorance is just as good as your knowledge"'.[6] Asimov was singling out the United States as particularly treacherous for intellectuals, although in truth the same predicament applies to every country, East and West, North and South.

Cicero: philo-politician

There is a curious puzzle that divides scholars on Cicero: was the great man a philosopher who happened to get lucky in politics, or was he a politician who only dabbed into philosophy when his political career came to an end? This is an important question, since the answer to it will determine the most propitious way to interpret the writings and actions of this historical figure.

Cicero pondered this question himself, towards the end of his life. He tells us, in no uncertain terms, that for him politics always came first, and that he focussed on philosophy only when he couldn't participate actively in politics. He goes as far as to say that 'I took the view that philosophy was a substitute for political activity'. This explains why in his biography of Cicero, Anthony Everitt stresses that 'Cicero is explicit that [his philosophical works] was an alternative to the public life from which he was barred.'[7] Furthermore, Cicero doesn't seem to think very highly of his own philosophical work, even claiming that there was 'nothing original in my philosophical work'. For someone known for his arrogance, such modesty is disconcerting. Cicero's superciliousness was legendary. There was no irony when he wrote in a letter to his friend Atticus: 'And what will history say of me a thousand years hence? I am far more in awe of that than of the tittle-tattle of my contemporaries.'[8] Cicero would be pleased that we are still reading his work 2,000 years hence, and that some of us continue to write books on him.

The chronology of events in Cicero's life adds support to his claim that for him politics always comes before philosophy, and doing philosophy is second-best to political action. This is also the view of Gesine Manuwald: 'Although Cicero regarded a thorough education, including philosophy, as a precondition for an accomplished orator and senior statesman ... he considered writing philosophical works as second-best ... and as a way of doing a service to the Republic when active intervention was not possible.'[9] He devoted himself to philosophy in the two periods in his life when he was banned from politics: in the mid to late 50 BC, when he was exiled from Rome, and in 46–44 BC when he returned to Rome but was barred by Julius Caesar from political activism.

In politics Cicero had a knack for always backing the wrong horse, an unfortunate habit that in Ancient Rome could seriously shorten your life expectancy.[10] Politics in Rome was a very personal affair, and people backed politicians the same way that punters place bets at the races. A political win translated into a windfall for its supporters, from protection to economic gains. But politics was a high-stakes game. Because many Roman politicians were also Roman generals, politics was indistinguishable from military campaigns and factions, which added an element of danger. During periods of civil war (Sulla vs. Marius; Caesar vs. Pompey; Brutus and Cassius vs. the triumvirate of Octavian, Marc Antony and Lepidus; Octavian vs. Marc Antony) neutrality was not an option, and the game of politics turned into a version of *Squid Game*, where losers (and their supporters) were eliminated, by death.[11]

When the civil war between Julius Caesar and Pompey broke out in 49 BC, Cicero joined Pompey's forces, but Pompey was defeated in war at Pharsalus and subsequently murdered. Many men were killed for much more trivial deeds than backing a losing general in civil war, but Cicero's life was spared by Julius Caesar on the understanding that he would no longer play any active role in politics.[12] Cicero duly obliged and turned to his philosophical writings.

The standard account suggests that for Cicero the only work which counts is in the service of the state; if it isn't political work, it simply isn't work at all.[13] In the preface to the second book of his *On Divination*, written around 44 BC, Cicero writes: 'For in my books I have become the speaker expressing his opinion in the senate and the politician addressing the assembled citizens, in the belief that philosophy had replaced my administration of the state.'[14] But notwithstanding Cicero's own views about his life and work, an alternative account can be constructed. Contrary to what may seem, and even contrary to what Cicero apparently said, with Cicero it is impossible to distinguish philosophy from politics. Cicero's engagement with politics was philosophy in action, and his philosophy was politics in theory.

Cicero belonged to a small group of senators and intellectuals who took philosophy extremely seriously. This elite party included Cato the Younger, Brutus, Varro, and Nigidius Figulus. Like them Cicero believed that philosophy laid the path to virtue, that philosophy was instrumental in bringing out the best in people: *quoniam philosophia vir bonus efficitur et fortis*, which translates 'for philosophy makes a man good and brave'. But what's more, Cicero saw philosophy as an 'extension' of his political life. As Catherine Steel says, his philosophical work ought to be treated as 'an aspect of, and not a substitute for, political activity'.[15]

The distinction between philosophy and politics mirrors the other well-known dichotomy between what in Latin is referred to as *otium* and *negotium*. Although these terms do not lend themselves to simple translations, *otium* is often translated as 'leisure time', although this should not be confused with idleness, which has derogatory connotations. *Otium* is the pursuit of activities beyond active public life, which is the meaning of *negotium*. Another way of making sense of this distinction is that *otium* tends to occur in the private sphere, whereas *negotium* is in the public sphere.

The difference between *otium* and *negotium* finds a powerful echo in Hannah Arendt's distinction between 'vita activa' and 'vita contemplativa': Arendt was a firm believer that active engagement, the life of action and speech, must form the basis for political life. However what is important to emphasize here is that *otium* and *negotium* should not be treated as a dichotomy, since politics and philosophy are not mutually exclusive categories. While politicking and philosophizing are different types of activities, with Cicero they become almost symbiotic, reinforcing one another. The best politicians are driven by a philosophical vision, and political philosophy is primarily the theoretical side of politics. Cicero's philosophically engaged politics, and his politically engaged philosophy, are two sides of the same coin.[16] This possibly explains why Cicero wrote extensively about truth, and ethics, but unlike Aristotle he had nothing to say about logic or the natural sciences.

At the same time, one must be careful to avoid what Katharina Volk refers to as the 'functionalist' approach, whereby in Roman times cultural pursuits, including philosophy, were not engaged for their own sake, 'but merely to fulfil ulterior social or political functions'.[17] Volk is absolutely right. However, in Cicero's case, it is very difficult to separate the philosopher from the politician, especially in his major works discussed in this book: *On Duties*, *On the Republic*, *On Old Age*, and *On Friendship*. When Cicero was engaged in his philosophical works, he wasn't just philosophizing for the sake of it; he was writing, debating his writings with friends, and distributing his written work. Cicero realized the importance of dissemination because, as Yelena Baraz reminds us, he firmly believed in 'the ability of philosophy to influence and improve people's characters and actions'.[18]

Cicero was not the first to recognize the transformative powers of political participation, Aristotle came to the same conclusion a few centuries before him. But for Cicero it has to be the right type of political participation, or at least political participation for the right reasons. This is where the importance of philosophy emerges. This is what sets Cicero apart from all the other political figures in Rome at the time. Cicero's philosophical writings were a form of political activism, a form of *negotium* via *otium*. When Cicero says that he wrote philosophy as a service to the well-being of the state, he is telling us that one cannot serve the state unless one is philosophically well-informed. Raphael Woolf makes the point that Cicero's philosophical output must be read against the backdrop of the tumultuous dying days of the Roman Republic 'leading as it does a special urgency to an abiding concern of his: the question of how philosophy can act as a force for good in the wider world'. Woolf is right when he says that Cicero's commensurate belief that philosophy ought not to be done in isolation from its wider social and political context 'is one of the most distinctive and poignant aspects of his philosophical approach'.[19]

In his major treatise on ethics, *On Duties*, which will be the subject of the next chapter, Cicero tells us that the pursuit of truth, which is one of our most pressing moral duties, should be our primary goal during periods of *otium*: 'Especially unique to man is the search and scrutiny into truth. This is why, when we are free from unavoidable business and concerns, we are eager to see, hear, and learn things. We reckon that the acquisition of knowledge of hidden or remarkable features is necessary for the happy life'.[20] Duties persist beyond our active public life, and are present even in our time of leisure; all this reinforces the idea that *otium* and *negotium* have a lot more in common than one may think.

It is a well-known fact that Cicero had a mild dislike, and strong distrust, for Julius Caesar. There are many passages where Cicero is highly critical of Caesar, even if his name is not mentioned, like this passage from his *On Duties*: 'But most men when fired by desire for military commands, high offices, or glory totally forget the claims of justice'.[21] What transpires here is the fact that Caesar had many talents, certainly as a military leader and strategist, and he even engaged in some scholarly activities, but he was not a philosopher. While there is no textual evidence, one is tempted to speculate that when it comes to philosophy Julius Caesar may have had an inferiority complex in respect to Cicero.[22]

The closest Julius Caesar came to writing something philosophical was his *Anticato*, which was a response to Cicero's *Cato*, a pamphlet in praise of the political and philosophical rigour of his friend Cato the Younger. But Caesar fails to engage with Cato's politics or philosophy, limiting himself to a very personal attack. One is left wondering whether Caesar was incapable to appreciate the virtues of the Roman Republic because he was unable to grasp the idea of the public good. It is only through philosophy that we come to realize our duty to the *res publica*, the public thing, and the public good. According to Cicero, without the guidance of philosophy, we can only pursue our own self-interest, which inevitably leads to corruption.

There were many powerful figures in Rome, like Marius, Sulla, Catiline, Pompey, Octavian and Julius Caesar, who were driven by the lust for wealth and glory, and in that sense, they were precursors of *Homo Oeconomicus*. Perhaps none more so than Marcus Licinius Crassus (ca. 115–53 BC), Rome's richest man who amassed his wealth from Sulla's proscription of opponents. Crassus was the first tycoon who bankrolled Julius Caesar's political career, an astute political player who understood that it was possible to exercise power through money.[23] Cicero on the other hand was driven by a strong sense of public ethics and public affairs, grounded on a philosophical vision: he was a *Homo Philosophicus*.

History tells us that Cicero's beloved Roman Republic was suppressed by Caesar's dictatorship, and consequentially *Homo Philosophicus* was crushed and replaced by *Homo Oeconumicus*, so much so that the idea of *Homo Philosophicus* is today a mere footnote in history. *Homo Oeconomicus* is now driving our civilization over the cliff, it is therefore time to reinstate *Homo Philosophicus*, time to restore the reputation of Cicero, and above all to restore the values and virtues of the *res publica* that was synonymous with Cicero's philosophical and political work.

Do philosophers make good politicians?

What makes Cicero a unique figure in the history of Ancient Rome, as well as Western civilization, is the combination of being a philosopher and a politician. This is a very rare combination. Martha Nussbaum is probably right when she warns us that 'we need to keep reminding ourselves that philosophers are not especially likely to be good politicians' and that 'the professional training of philosophers makes them ill-suited to a world of political action'.[24] Nussbaum is (almost) prepared to make an exception for Cicero, who she singles out together with Seneca, Marcus Aurelius and Karl Marx as offering 'distinguished examples of the combination', although she admonishes Cicero for sometimes losing the characteristic philosophical virtues of precision, self-containment, and reflectiveness when he entered politics. What Nussbaum perhaps doesn't appreciate is that Cicero was always his own harshest critic.[25]

In this chapter I have contended that the secret to Cicero's political acumen was his philosophical wisdom, and that he remains a role model for both inspiring politicians and philosophers. But admittedly this is a controversial view not shared by many scholars of Cicero over many centuries. One of Cicero's first critics was also one of his biggest admirers, namely the Italian scholar and poet Francesco Petrarca (Petrarch). It is a little-known fact that during the Middle Ages Cicero was more influential, and more widely read, than Aristotle.[26] In 1345, Petrarch discovered in a library in Verona Cicero's letters to his friend Atticus. This was a momentous event in intellectual history, with this discovery often credited with nothing less than kick-starting the Renaissance. But Petrarch was disappointed by what he read, developing a more critical view of Cicero as a result. In particular, Petrarch accused Cicero of inconsistency and even fickleness: 'While I expressed admiration for Cicero, almost without reservation, as a man whom I loved and honoured above all others, and amazement too at his golden eloquence and his heavenly genius, I found at the same time a little fault with his fickleness and inconsistency, traits that are revealed everywhere in his life and works.'[27]

The great nineteenth-century German scholar Theodor Mommsen has gone down in history as one of Cicero's harshest critics. Following in the footsteps of the German classical historian Wilhelm Karl August Drumann (1786–1861), who also vigorously detested Cicero's alleged spinelessness, Mommsen published his highly influential *History of Rome* in three volumes between 1854 and 1856. This literary feat earned him the Nobel Prize in Literature in 1902. In it Mommsen has this to say about Cicero the politician: 'As a statesman without insight, idea, or purpose, he figured successively as democrat, as aristocrat, and as a tool of the monarchs, and was never more than a short-sighted egotist.'[28] Mommsen also accuses Cicero of being a coward, suggesting that in the rare occasions when he was persuaded to act decisively, he did so 'like all cowards anxiously endeavouring to avoid the appearance of cowardice, and yet trembling before the formidable responsibility.'[29] Mommsen's opinion of Cicero the philosopher is equally uncompromising: 'In the character of an author, on the other hand, he stands quite as low as in that of a statesman ... he was in fact as thoroughly a dabbler, that it was pretty much a matter of indifference to what work he applied his hand. By nature a journalist in the worst sense of the term – abounding, as he himself says, in words, poor beyond all conception in ideas.'[30]

Poor Cicero. But why so much animosity? What did Cicero do to upset Mommsen? It is possible that Mommsen's dismissive assessment of Cicero was driven by a political agenda, due to Cicero's obstinate defence of the Roman Republic. The fact that Mommsen refers to Cicero's beloved Republic as a bankrupt commonwealth gives it away. Nicholas Cole is right to speculate that the devastating critique of Cicero by authors like Mommsen must be read in conjunction with the re-evaluation of Julius Caesar: 'Mommsen's account criticizes the champion of a bankrupt republic dominated by a corrupt aristocracy so that he can praise Caesar, presented by him as a statesman with the vision to reform the Republic's ills.'[31] Mommsen, writing in the nineteenth century, was blinded by the appeal for the strong man, the uncompromising leader and the authoritarian character. Mommsen had no time for *Homo Philosophicus*, instead he craved for *Homo Fortissimus*.[32]

In the nineteenth century the great German philosopher Georg Wilhelm Friedrich Hegel was star-struck by Julius Caesar, as was Napoleon. In the twentieth-century Julius Caesar inspired

Mussolini's Fascism. Romano Mussolini, Benito Mussolini's son, was asked a few years ago who was his father's great example in history, with whom did Benito Mussolini identify himself? Romano Mussolini answered: 'He admired many historical characters, maybe above all Caesar.'[33] Between 1880 and 1930 there was a concerted effort by those sympathetic to a return to dictatorship to silence Cicero and his admirers, so much so that as Philippe Rousselot explains, Cicero was the object of wholehearted adulation by the moderate political class and by the Left. In this period Cicero became the emblem of the 'Republic of Lawyers' at a time when the rule of law was under siege.[34] It is therefore not surprising that in the twenty-first century, as the far-right makes inroads on the global political scene, Caesarism still casts a long shadow on politics while Cicero remains undiscovered.[35]

The general perception of Ancient Rome is often romanticized, being fundamentally different from the historical reality. We like to think of Rome as the epitome of civilization, a term used to capture the conceptual antithesis of barbarism. Civilization stands for reason, dialogue, honesty, ethics, whereas barbarism settles disputes through violence, brutality, where moral concern is conspicuous by its absence, and human affairs are conducted on animalistic premises. The truth is somewhere in the messy middle of this dichotomy.

There is no doubt that intellectuals, and philosophers in particular, were key players during the final tumultuous years of the Roman Republic, often occupying the centre stage. This was a time when, as Katharina Volk reminds us in her superb book on that period, some of the most important intellectuals were also leading politicians: it was not only a case that their writings were influenced by their political views, but their public actions were motivated by their intellectual views.[36] This was certainly true of Cicero, but also of others amongst his contemporaries including M. Iunius Brutus.

Brutus has gone down in history as Julius Caesar's vile assassin, the man who betrayed his friend, and stabbed to death one of history's greatest idols. History has not been kind to Brutus. Much maligned by Shakespeare, Dante, and countless others over the centuries, we forget that Brutus was also an accomplished philosopher, author of an influential treatise on ethics, *De Virtute*, a work that was greatly admired by Cicero.[37] His defining political action was, in Cicero's view, a courageous act of virtue.

But history is more often than not made by people dexterous with swords, not words, and Rome was not an exception to this rule. As Richard Alston reminds us, Rome at the time was a predatory state, its power resting on violence. And the violence in Rome was often shocking, and certainly not confined to gladiatorial games. During the political conflict between two elected politicians, tribune Gaius Gracchus and consul Lucius Opimius in 121 BC, the latter ordered the death of Gracchus and oversaw the execution of 3,000 of his supporters. He offered a rich reward to the person who brought him Gracchus's head: the weight of the head in gold. The head that was brought to him was unusually heavy; it turns out that the brain had been removed and replaced with lead. This is how Plutarch narrates the story:

> Someone cut off the head of Caius [Gracchus], we are told, and was carrying it along, but was robbed of it by a certain friend of

Opimius, Septimuleius; for proclamation had been made at the beginning of the battle that an equal weight of gold would be paid the men who brought the head of Caius or Fulvius. Septimuleius stuck the head of Caius on a spear and brought it to Opimius, and when it was placed in a balance it weighed seventeen pounds and two thirds, since Septimuleius, besides showing himself to be a scoundrel, had also perpetrated a fraud; for he had taken out the brain and poured melted lead in its place.[38]

Stories of this nature were not unusual in Ancient Rome, in fact they were the norm in those times. It may be necessary to rethink the essence of Roman politics and society, as Richard Alston says, 'starting not from the speeches and philosophical discourses of Cicero and his friends ... but from the perspective of the soldier in the camp, or the poor man in the street or the field.'[39] Philosophy plays its part in the way history unfolds, but violence remains the predominant force.

Roman society was not ready for someone like Cicero, and notwithstanding his considerable achievements Cicero remained a misfit. I would like to think that things have improved since then. Outside of universities philosophers are not being welcomed with open arms, in fact even within some universities their existence is precarious and philosophy departments constantly struggle for their survival. But at least today we have come to recognize that democracy is both an idea and an ideal, and that philosophy is required to support and sustain our democratic institutions. I think Cicero understood this before anyone else. Perhaps philosophy can prevent our democracy from ending up like the Roman Republic. This is why philosophy matters; this is why Cicero still matters.

Conclusion

Cicero belongs to a very rare breed of human beings, one at risk of extinction – today, like in Ancient Rome, there are very few politically active philosophers, and even fewer philosophically inclined politicians. Cicero was not simply an outstanding philosopher and politician; he was a better philosopher because of his experience in politics, and his political leadership was enlightened by his philosophical interests.

During the nineteenth century Cicero's stock price went down, while Julius Caesar's went up. In the subsequent 100 years, especially around the 1920s and 1930s, Cicero became totally overshadowed by Caesar, and even today Caesar remains a household name while Cicero is being relegated to a footnote in history, except for a small gang of hardcore Ciceronians. J. Balsdon's exuberant claim that Cicero was 'perhaps the most civilized man who has ever lived' is very much a dissenting opinion.[40] This book wants to revert this trend in an effort to suggest that history needs to re-assess Cicero, and politics needs to learn from Cicero, look up to him as a role model.

Malcolm Schofield suggests that according to Cicero the best qualification for writing political philosophy is political experience at the highest level.[41] He is right. Unlike 2,000 years ago it is now possible to be a 'professional' political philosopher, and there are scores of political philosophers teaching in universities around the world. But political philosophers today are not expected or required to have any political experience, at any level, and many of them even have contempt for political science, or any empirical methodology applied to the study of politics, which is unforgivable. At the same time, the vast majority of professional politicians have no interest in political philosophy, and some even hide their intellectual curiosity for fear that it may damage their political careers. This is a sad state of affairs, which is precisely why the world needs more people like Cicero, more philosopher-politicians, more *Homo Philosophicus*, and most of all it needs to get over the dangerous hype of the strong military leader personified by Julius Caesar and his many imitators.

2

Politics as ethics

No phase of life, whether public or private, can be free from duty
MARCUS TULLIUS CICERO (ON DUTIES)

Some writers write very little, either out of choice or life circumstances, perhaps only one book, and subsequently their name is forever associated with their one, outstanding labour of love. This is the case with Emily Brontë's *Wuthering Heights*, Harper Lee's *To Kill a Mockingbird*, or J. D. Salinger's *The Catcher in the Rye*. In philosophy, Michael de Montaigne's *Essays* comes to mind. Sometimes even if an author publishes many books, one work stands out from all others, and they will forever be remembered (rightly or wrongly) for their one literary achievement, whether they like it or not. This is the fate of Herman Melville's *Moby Dick*, and in philosophy Thomas Hobbes's *Leviathan*.

When authors write many books, all important in their own ways, the jury is out on which one book best captures the essence of their contribution to knowledge. In a thought experiment inspired by BBC Radio 4's Desert Island Discs, if one can only rescue one book from the complete works of one author, what would that *magnum opus* be? Only one book from John Steinbeck, *East of Eden* or *The Grapes of Wrath*? One book from Karl Marx, *The 1844 Manuscripts* or *Capital*? One book from Ayn Rand ... perhaps in her case we will let the waves destroy the whole lot.

Consider for example the American philosopher John Rawls, arguably the most original and influential political philosopher of the last 150 years. I would be inclined to think that he should be judged, and remembered, for his first major masterpiece, *A Theory of Justice*, and not for the works he published after 1971, but of course not everyone would agree.[1] The same could be said for Descartes' *Discourse on the Method*, although his *Meditations on First Philosophy* must be given close consideration. Debating which one book, and one book only, to choose from the likes of *Rousseau* or *Locke* or *Kant* is the sort of exercise that could break friendships, if not start academic wars.

But what about Cicero? Is there one defining text that, more than all the others, captures his philosophical outlook? In my view, there is one text, amongst Cicero's many philosophical works, that best captures Cicero's essence, and therefore demands our special attention. This is the text where Cicero puts forward a grounding idea that can be found, in some shape or form, in all his other works; that helps to explain his decisions in politics; and that makes it easier to understand the man behind his letters, his speeches, his other philosophical texts. The text in question is *De Officiis* (On Duties).

The title *De Officiis* comes from the Latin term *officium*, which can be translated as duty, obligation, responsibility, or even commitment. The standard English translation of the title of this text is *On Duties*, although it is at times translated as *On Obligations*.[2] Cicero wrote *On Duties* in 44 BC, a few months after the death of Julius Caesar and a year before Cicero's own murder. Politics was a dangerous line of business in Ancient Rome, with success and premature death often being two sides of the same coin. Cicero was aware of this, as he survived several attempted assassinations during his life. But he persevered with his political project of saving the Roman Republic notwithstanding the risks to himself and his family, out of a sense of duty. The title might point to ethics, but in fact *On Duties* is perhaps Cicero's principal political treatise, to be read in conjunction with his other works *On the Republic* and *On Laws*.[3]

The duties Cicero is referring to in this text are specifically our moral duties. He is interested in understanding the nature of our duties to morality, hence why one should act morally even when non-moral behaviour is more advantageous, either because it is less risky or simply more lucrative. As Cicero famously said, 'Only he lives freely who finds joy in the performance of his duties.' Whatever his faults, and he had many, Cicero tried to live according to this principle. He lived the life he preached, and there are not many people in politics (or even outside politics) who can honestly say the same for themselves.

On Duties: An overview

Cicero wrote *On Duties* in the form of a letter to his son, Marcus Tullius Cicero Minor, who at the time was in Greece allegedly to study, although from what we know from reading Cicero's letters hedonism had a much stronger pull on Cicero the Younger than

Stoicism. Hence a fatherly reminder of what duties are, and why we should abide by them.

The text is divided into three books. The first book centres around the idea of 'honour', which at the time of Cicero was closely related to ethics, and its four major foundations: the search for truth; the maintenance of social relations; fortitude; and *decorum*. The second book explores the idea of utility, while the third book considers the clash between honour (morality) and utility. Regarding this clash, Cicero had a very clear idea of how this should pan out when he writes: 'Let it be set down as an established principle, then, that what is morally wrong can never be expedient.'[4] Cicero's admonition speaks to us, and one suspects that he would not be impressed by the world we have created 2,000 years since he wrote this text. In what follows we will concentrate only on Book One, which even Cicero himself considered to be the most important of the three books.

Book One starts with a distinction between two types of duties: 'absolute' and 'intermediate'. This echoes a distinction introduced by Immanuel Kant in the eighteenth century, which all students of moral philosophy are familiar with, between 'perfect' and 'imperfect' duties. It is curious how Kant's terminology has become dominant, while Cicero's has almost been forgotten, notwithstanding the similarities. We also know that Kant was an admirer of Cicero, and was familiar with Cicero's work.

Perfect or absolute duties allow for no exception, whereas intermediate duties, as Cicero says, are practical guidelines for conducting our lives, based on plausible rather than ideal justification. Cicero quickly brushes aside considerations of absolute or perfect duties, wanting to concentrate instead on imperfect or intermediate duties. Following in Plato's footsteps, Cicero then introduces the four cardinal virtues: wisdom, justice, courage, and temperance. In fact, Cicero is interested in discussing only the first two virtues, wisdom and justice, but he adds an interesting twist to these virtues: Cicero interprets wisdom in terms of our duty to seek truth, and justice as our duty to maintain social relations.

These virtues apply to both political leaders and ordinary citizens. Being an elected official, holding a position of power, puts one under special duties, but in fact for Cicero in a republic *everyone* has obligations, towards each other and towards the republic. In other words, Cicero is as concerned with the 'good citizen' as he is with the 'good statesman'. After all, in the Roman Republic all statesmen were also citizens, and all citizens could aspire to become statesmen. Cicero is keen to reinforce a paradigm of equality, the lifeblood of a healthy republic. Perhaps in stressing the equality of a just republic Cicero was also taking a dig at Julius Caesar, who circulated the myth that he was a semi-god, a descendant of the goddess Venus.

During Julius Caesar's funeral a bright object was seen shooting across the sky, an omen interpreted as evidence that Caesar had joined the gods. This was nothing more than an astronomical phenomenon, a comet (today known as *Sidus Iulium* or Julian Star, which was seen in Rome and China), but in one of the earliest recorded examples of political spin Julius Caesar's adopted nephew Gaius Octavius perpetrated this legend to reinforce the message that he was Caesar's heir and successor. Cicero had very little time for any mystical nonsense, which he considered politically toxic. He probably had his tongue firmly in his cheek when in his speech *Pro Marcello* (46 BC), Cicero writes that Julius Caesar is blessed with almost godlike wisdom: 'For I cannot by any means pass over in silence such great humanity, such unprecedented and unheard-of clemency, such moderation in the exercise of supreme and universal power, such incredible and almost godlike wisdom.'[5]

Our duty to truth

Given the nature of the subject, namely our duties or obligations, one would be tempted to assume that Cicero followed in the footsteps of other Stoic philosophers, but this would be wrong. Stoics were idealists, holding impossibly high standards, only interested in 'perfect' wisdom. Cicero on the other hand was a realist, and wanted morality to be attainable for everyone. According to Cicero we can all be good, or at least good enough for the republic, and it is our duty to work on being good citizens.

The fact that Cicero, on the question of virtue, is influenced by and yet critical of Stoicism is something worth emphasizing. On other issues, for example when he discusses death, he is not afraid to lean towards Epicurean doctrines. This is not because Cicero was philosophically fickle, or confused, but because Cicero subscribed to the school of thought known as the New Academy, characterized by its position on scepticism. Cicero's philosophical outlook allows him to agree with a school of thought on one issue, and with a different school of thought on another issue. This explains why on ethical matters Cicero is not opposed to certain aspects of Stoicism, and while he is critical of the dogmatism and impossibly high standards demanded by Stoicism, like other Stoic philosophers before him

Cicero believes that to live an ethical life, with honour, is to live in harmony with our human nature. Cicero even engages with the idea that virtue is sufficient for living a happy life, which was the central thesis of Brutus's philosophical work *Virtue*. Brutus was a follower of the Old Academy.

This idea of living in harmony with human nature allows Cicero to explore a favourite topic of many philosophers over the past two millennia: human nature. More specifically, Cicero asks what makes us, human beings, different from other animals. Philosophers have been pondering this question for millennia. For example, in the *Economic Manuscripts of 1844*, Marx writes that apart from producing for the sake of survival, man creates also according to the 'laws of beauty', making aesthetics for the sake of it a distinctive feature of human nature. Cicero considers a few different options, but the most compelling one, and the one he spends more time on, is our disposition to seek out truth, or as Cicero puts it 'above all, the search after truth and its eager pursuit are peculiar to men'.[6]

For Cicero the quest for truth is peculiar to humankind, so much so that he considers the pursuit of truth a fundamental moral duty. Truth is not just an issue in epistemology or metaphysics, it is also a moral imperative. Hence the reason why the opposite of truth, namely deception and dishonesty, are morally unacceptable. If he were living today, I'm certain that Cicero would consider the growing cancer of post-truth as not only misguided, and dangerous, but also morally objectionable.[7]

The idea that citizens have a duty to do their best to hold beliefs that are true, or very likely to be true, is something we will return to in the Epilogue. This idea that we all have responsibilities as believers is generally associated with the seventeenth-century philosopher John Locke. It is also known in the literature as the 'alethic obligation', from the Greek term for truth, Aletheia (ἀλήθεια).[8] It is worth pointing out that many centuries before Locke, Cicero made this obligation the centre piece of his ethical system. And as Cicero reminds us, whether it's public or private life, nothing is devoid of moral obligations.

Before we leave the topic of truth, there is an important point worth stressing that is crucial for a correct reading of Cicero's moral and political philosophy. Cicero argued for a duty to truth, not a duty to *the* truth. This is a fundamental distinction. As a Natural Law philosopher, partially influenced by Stoicism, it would be tempting to assume that Cicero had a fully worked-out idea of the truth from which he deduced all his moral principles. But that's not the case. Cicero had a pragmatist view of truth. The next section will take a quick detour, focussing on one of Cicero's lesser-known works on epistemology, *The Academics*, which deals explicitly with his views on truth and scepticism, before we return to our analysis of his morality in *On Duties*.

Scepticism and pragmatism

In the history of philosophy Pragmatism is generally associated with the work of three leading American philosophers writing between the end of the nineteenth century and the early twentieth century: C. S. Peirce, William James, and John Dewey. In the late twentieth century two other American philosophers took over their mantle: Hilary

Putnam and Richard Rorty. All this points to a single fact: pragmatism is as American as apple pie. And yet, a Roman philosopher writing 2,000 years before them could possibly be their intellectual predecessor, making him the first (non-)American pragmatist.

Pragmatism has a defining position on the nature of truth: namely, that there are no external truths, no absolute facts which exist independent of human experience. For a pragmatist, truth does not correspond with an abstracted objective reality, instead truth is what coheres with particular systems of belief. This is also arguably the major difference between Plato and Cicero, as pointed out by Alan Ryan: 'Where Plato sees us pulled toward the depth of philosophical truth, Cicero embeds us in concentric circles of social connections.'[9]

There are, of course, many varieties of Pragmatism. According to Canadian philosopher Cheryl Misak, a proposition is true if it is what is best for the community of enquirers to believe, where 'best' refers to that which best fits with the evidence and argument.[10] It would be tempting, but ultimately erroneous, to associate the idea of what is *best* for the community of enquirers to believe, with what is most *useful* for them to believe. William James is widely criticized, including by fellow pragmatists, for associating the idea of what is 'best' with what is 'useful'. James even goes as far as to say that truth is to be pursued precisely because it 'pays' to pursue the truth, but this position is untenable. Instead, the central and most persuasive insight of Pragmatism is that there is a connection between truth and the practical business of enquiry. What is best for a community of enquirers is the best that enquiry can do, and as Misak reminds us, in the political domain this practical business of enquiry takes the form of deliberation, agreement, debate, and reflection.

Cicero's pragmatism had an epistemological core, which can be traced to his advocacy of scepticism. It is important to stress that not all pragmatist philosophers embrace scepticism. For example, although Peirce endorsed fallibilism, he refuted scepticism. But in Cicero's case scepticism and pragmatism seem to go hand-in-hand. Cicero's aim in writing the *The Academics* was to justify the sceptical criticism of the New Academy, later to be known as the school of Academic scepticism. This school was founded and developed by philosophers who mean little to us today, like Arcesilaus, Carneades, and Philo of Larissa, but their ideas are still alive today thanks to Cicero.

Philosophically speaking, perhaps the biggest influence of the New Academy on Cicero's philosophical outlook is the fact that Cicero does not seek *certainty*, instead he is satisfied with the *probable*. Philosophical doubt, or scepticism, allows for the probable to overshadow the certain. This is what Cicero says, making the point that the purpose of any discussion is to bring to light 'something which is either true or approaches as closely as possible the truth'.[11] He goes on to explain that while some people have no doubt about the essential truth of the doctrines they maintain, 'we hold many theories to be probable, and can readily act upon them, though we can scarcely state them dogmatically'.[12] And in *De Natura Deorum* (On the Nature of the Gods), from 45 BC, Cicero writes: 'We academics are not the type of philosophers who think that nothing is true ....Our view [is] that many things are *probable*, and that though these are not demonstrably true they guide the life of the wise man, because they are so significant and clear-cut.'[13] Cicero comments that embracing scepticism gives one more freedom, being unshackled from the constraints of dogmatism.

The distinction between what is believed to be certain, as opposed to what is probable, is crucial in Cicero. He wants us to think about truth in terms of what is merely probable, where the probable is nothing more than what is likely to be true. Walter Nicgorski perfectly captures Cicero's position when he writes: 'The probable for Cicero is the likely true ... the probable is literally that which is able to be accepted (approved) as likely to be true. Thus Cicero effectively accepts as true, not however as certain and beyond philosophical doubt, whatever is probable.'[14]

For Cicero, the method of philosophical enquiry, grounded on philosophical deliberation and debate, is our best hope to recognize and agree on what is most probably true. Furthermore, Cicero's philosophical pragmatism is also the foundation of his political pragmatism. His political ambitions are motivated by the search for truth, but only in terms of what is probable. In other words, Cicero does not believe that politics is the implementation of an *a priori* philosophical system fully worked out independently of political contingencies. As Walter Nicgorski says, 'Cicero was clearly and persistently critical of the tendency of philosophical men to withdraw from the political arena and its responsibilities, and it can be incontestably inferred that he rejects as ill-founded any pretensions to settle those primary questions of metaphysics and theology as a condition and basis for applications to morals and politics'.[15] Cicero commends a *philosophical statesmanship*, but one driven by pragmatism.

Our civic duties

Back to Cicero's *On Duties*. After our duty to seek truth, Cicero suggests that the second foundation of morality is the maintenance of social order and communal living among men. There are, according to Cicero, two principal ways to safeguarding bonds among humans, and build trust across a community: via justice, and via generosity (kindness).

On the issue of justice, Cicero makes one of his most insightful comments, which is as powerful today as it was 2,000 years ago: 'The foundation of justice is trust [*fides*], in other words consistency and truthfulness in declarations and compacts.'[16] In the Loeb Classical Library edition, *De Officiis* (Book One, 23), *fides* is translated as 'good faith', but I personally prefer 'trust', since this term does a better job of capturing the idea of truth and fidelity to promises and agreements. Trust is the backbone of any civilized society. It is also the backbone of any democracy. Trust can conveniently be best described as 'encapsulated interest', the idea being that we place our trust in institutions, or persons, whom we believe to have strong reasons to act in our best interests, and who want to maintain a relationship with us.[17] Without trust, there is no civil society, there is only the state of nature.[18]

Thomas Hobbes in 1651 famously described the state of nature as the most abysmal place to live, where life is 'solitary, poor, nasty, brutish, and short' (*nota bene:* life is 'brutish' in the Hobbesian state of nature, not 'British', as one of my students once wrote in an exam). The Hobbesian state of nature is not to be understood historically, as a situation that was peculiar to a time in the distant past, but logically, as a possible future state of affairs. Hobbes's genius was to realize that the first casualty of reverting back to a state of nature is trust. He understood that without trust there is 'no place for industry, no knowledge of the face of the earth; no account of time; no arts; no letters; no society'.[19] Trust is inestimable, and irreplaceable, perhaps the most precious social capital a person or society can wish for. But trustworthiness is built very slowly over a long period of time, even though it can be lost instantly. As we saw in Chapter One, in our modern society, where *Homo Oeconomicus* roams unchallenged with unbridled personal ambition and avarice, levels of trust have never been so low. Human cooperation relies on trust, and where trust has been eroded, social cooperation falters. Trust and social cooperation are the driving forces of our greatest achievements.

Hobbes's state of nature captures an aspect of reality present in Ancient Rome at the end of the Republic and in today's advanced capitalist society. Just like in Hobbes's state of nature, in Ancient Rome there were two cardinal vices: violence and fraud. The same two cardinal vices are major forces dictating life in our advanced capitalist society. Cicero lived his life fighting against these vices, and his *On Duties* is a testament to his strong sense of morality, public and private. That's why the twenty-first century needs Cicero: we need to go back to the basics of morality and obligation, and we need to find the moral force to resist violence and fraud. In our present predicament, we could do a lot worse than to rediscover Cicero's *On Duties*.[20]

Justice

The Latin word for justice is *ius*, but this term is notoriously difficult to translate, in part because of its conceptual overlap with legal notions, although it is different from mere laws (*lex*). Malcolm Schofield perfectly captures the legal dimension of justice while retaining the distinction between *ius* (justice) and *lex* (law): 'This is justice or right as guaranteed by law ... with the implication that law – provided it is without arbitrariness – is what makes justice work as justice, through ensuring equal treatment for those subject to it.'[21]

Law has an important function within this conception of justice, namely, to create the trust that turns a group of strangers into a community. That is ultimately what justice is for Cicero: a system that binds the citizens association together, creating a communal sense of purpose and engendering the idea of the common good.[22] But in order for the trust to bind the citizens together, equality is essential. It is for this reason that Cicero champions an egalitarian conception of justice, although Cicero fails to appreciate that in a just society the equality cannot be only formal (legal and institutional) but also needs to be substantive (economic). I will return to the limitations and lacunas in Cicero's political theory, especially on issues of economic justice, in Chapter 6.

The idea of justice as constitutive of a community is a recurring theme in Cicero's writing. In his *On the Republic* (1.39), the topic of the next chapter, Cicero coins the phrase 'the consensus of justice' (*consensus iuris*) to capture the idea of justice as a communal enterprise where the people are 'brought together by legal consent [*consensus iuris*] and community of interest [*utilitatis communion sociatus*]'. The latter concept, '*utilitatis communion sociatus*', can be translated as either 'community of interest' or 'sharing in advantage'. For political philosophers familiar with John Rawls's theory of social justice, there seems to be an echo between what Cicero says here, and Rawls's wording that social justice combines elements of impartiality as well as mutual advantage, although unlike Rawls, Cicero was not endorsing a social contract.[23]

In the history of political thought, the social contract tradition we associate with Hobbes, Locke, Rousseau and Rawls articulates a unanimous, hypothetical agreement that uses the concept of a state of nature to explain key features of civil society, from the political legitimacy of the state to principles of social justice. There is no mention of the state of nature in Cicero's work, therefore Cicero is not a social contract theorist. Perhaps not surprisingly Hobbes was openly critical of Cicero.[24] However, the terminology of contractual law is integral to Cicero's argument. For Cicero the Roman citizen community (*civitas*) is framed by law, grounded on a partnership of legal contracts (*societas*). Contractual law is the bond that links citizens together, the invisible substructure of any republic. Violence being the opposite of law, it weakens our common bond, destroys our sense of community, and ultimately undermines the *res publica*. As Jill Harries explains, the legal character of *societas* must be understood as a contract based on consensus: 'Every element required for the legal partnership contract [must] be present. The people are designated the owners of the *res publica*, which is their shared asset, and the people themselves are partners with each other, having deliberately agreed to the contract, with the aim of benefiting or profiting from it.'[25]

In *On Duties* (Book 1, 22) Cicero does not use the term 'consensus of justice', but he returns to the idea of the importance of binding a human community, except that this time the emphasis is on the moral and political obligations of all citizens to make this happen. This is one of Cicero's most celebrated statements, and is worth quoting in full:

> *We are not born for ourselves alone,* but our country claims a share of our being, and our friends a share; and since, as the Stoics hold, everything that the earth produces is created for man's use; and as men, too, are born for the sake of men, that they may be able mutually to help one another; in this direction we ought to follow Nature as our guide, to contribute to the general good by an interchange of acts of kindness, by giving and receiving, and thus by our skill, our industry, and our talents to cement human society more closely together, man to man.[26]

What transpires here is Cicero's sense of justice as reciprocity, and our duty to others. In Cicero's work one will not find a theory of human rights, but there are the fundamentals of a theory of human duties.

Injustice

On Duties is an important text also for another reason, since here we find an account of injustice, a topic of timeless interest, even though contemporary political philosophers have become obsessed with defining the key principles of social justice while paying less attention to the nature of injustice.[27]

Cicero tells us that greed, which can take the form of lust for money or for glory, is the source of all injustice: 'But, for the most part, people are led to wrong-doing in order to secure some personal end; in this vice, avarice is generally the controlling motive.'[28] Here the Latin term *iniuriam* is translated as 'wrong-doing', but I think 'injustice' might give a better sense of what Cicero is telling us. Thomas Habinek offers this translation of the same sentence: 'The primary reason people commit injustice is to obtain something they desire: greed is often manifest in such cases.'[29]

Cicero's claim that greed is the source of injustice also applies to our modern society, today. Our consumer-obsessed society may have accentuated this, but things were not much different in Ancient Rome, and Cicero was already aware of the link between consumerism and injustice: 'Fine establishments and the comforts of life in elegance and abundance also afford pleasure, and the desire to secure it gives rise to the insatiable thirst for wealth.'[30]

As for those who seek glory, Cicero is equally unimpressed: 'The great majority of people, however, when they fall a prey to ambition for either military or civil authority, are carried away by it so completely that they quite lose sight of the claims of justice.'[31] As often the case with Cicero, he has specific people in mind when he makes accusations, and he is not afraid to name names. In this case, his target is Julius Caesar: 'now in the effrontery of Gaius Caesar, who, to gain that sovereign power which by a depraved imagination he had conceived in his fancy, trod underfoot all laws of gods and men.'[32] And Cicero could see through Caesar's celebrated disposition for clemency:

We may also observe that a great many people do many things that seem to be inspired more by a spirit of ostentation than by heartfelt kindness; for such people are not really generous but are rather influenced by a sort of ambition to make a show of being openhanded. Such a pose is nearer akin to hypocrisy than to generosity or moral goodness.[33]

There is also another aspect of Cicero's analysis of injustice that makes his work *On Duties* still extremely relevant to us today. For Cicero an injustice can take two forms: as direct, intentional wrongdoing, or as mere indifference to suffering caused by injustice: 'There are, on the other hand, two kinds of injustice – the one, on the part of those who inflict wrong, the other on the part of those who, when they can, do not shield from wrong those upon whom it is being inflicted.'[34] The second type of injustice is particularly interesting. What Cicero is telling us here is captured by 'passive injustice', a concept that has seen a resurgence of interest in contemporary political philosophy. In her 1988 Storrs Lecturer at Yale Law School, Judith Shklar reminds us that apart from acts of direct or active injustice, we must also consider cases of passive injustice: 'Passive injustice is a strictly civic notion … passive injustice refers to our public roles. … The passively unjust man … is simply indifferent to what goes on around him, especially when he sees fraud and violence.'[35]

Shklar is absolutely right to point out that passive injustice is a crucial concept for a comprehensive understanding of the phenomenon of social injustice, something that Cicero was already addressing in 44 BC when he wrote *On Duties*. The affinity between Cicero and Shklar is not accidental: Shklar was very familiar with Cicero's work, and just like Cicero, the idea of citizens' duties is pivotal to Shklar's political theory.

Conclusion

Cicero's major contribution to philosophy is in the area of moral philosophy, and *On Duties* is his clearest statement. In Book 1, Cicero highlights two key concepts: truth and justice. These two concepts are strongly intertwined in Cicero's moral architecture: we have a duty to truth, and a duty to justice. This way of thinking about ethics is still powerful, and relevant, especially in the present climate of post-truth rhetoric.

In Cicero's ethical theory, justice has a strong communitarian flavour, but with an egalitarian twist. He reasoned for a duty to maintain social order, where justice forms a communal bond. Furthermore, equality is intrinsic to Cicero's sense of republican justice. The Roman Republic gave Roman citizens a set of rights that did not exist prior to its inception, and this idea of rights is still central to our political endeavours. It is not a coincidence that our modern conception of democracy still finds in the Roman Republic a distant but powerful source of inspiration. But apart from our rights, Cicero also wanted to instil in us a sense of duty, towards others and our polity. Hence Cicero's idea of justice as consensus is built on reciprocity and forged on the common good.

But unlike the Greek philosophers that Cicero greatly admired, principally Plato, in *On Duties* Cicero does not speculate about justice as an abstract ideal, instead he offers a realistic picture starting from the non-ideal concept of injustice. In Book 3 Cicero puts forward a moral argument that could be used today against modern capitalism, especially the way the capitalist mode of production undermines the spirit of solidarity in a community:

For a man to take something from his neighbour and to profit by his neighbour's loss is more contrary to Nature than is death or poverty or pain or anything else that can affect either our person or our property. For, in the first place, injustice is fatal to social life and fellowship between man and man. For, if we are so disposed that each, to gain some personal benefit, will defraud or injure his neighbour, then those bonds of human society, which are most in accord with Nature's laws, must of necessity be broken.[36]

Cicero's views on injustice, and ethics, express sentiments that we find, many centuries later, in the works of Jean-Jacques Rousseau and the young Karl Marx. His message that the pursuit of selfish, individual interests risk undermining the common good, destroying the republic, and with it all those fragile institutions which we rely upon for communal living, is still as valid today as it was 2,000 years ago.

3

The people's republic

We are born for justice, and what is just is based, not on opinion,
but on objective reality

MARCUS TULLIUS CICERO (ON LAWS)

'Civic Republicanism' is one of the hottest political ideas in contemporary political philosophy. This idea has nothing to do with the Republican Party in the United States. The political philosophy of Civic Republicanism is a very old idea that goes back to Ancient Greece and Ancient Rome, thus it predates American politics, and the politics of liberalism and neo-liberalism, by many centuries. In that sense there is nothing new about Civic Republicanism *per se*, but the revival of this old tradition in the last two decades is one of the most exciting developments in political philosophy, especially as it poses a strong challenge to the hegemony of liberalism.

There are important overlaps between the traditions of liberalism and republicanism in political thought, as we shall see, but for the time being it may be useful to keep these two ideologies apart, to the extent that liberalism and republicanism offer two different interpretations of the meaning and functioning of democracy. The type of democracy we are accustomed to in the West, and very much take for granted, is liberal democracy. Undoubtedly, liberal democracy has many virtues, but it also has its limitations, and some disturbing blind spots.[1] Civic Republicanism invites us to imagine what democracy could be, and perhaps should be, as an alternative to the liberal paradigm.

Cicero's political philosophy is of the republican variety, and his lessons on the best way to organize political affairs are still valid today. Even after many centuries, Cicero's political acumen remains enlightening and revolutionary. This chapter will start with a brief overview of the political philosophy of Civic Republicanism in general, with special emphasis on the republican ideas of citizenship, domination and arbitrariness. This will be followed by an analysis of the striking similarities between the major threats we face today in our liberal democracy, and those faced by Romans in Cicero's time. Finally, we will explore the modern-day relevance of Cicero's text *On the Republic*.

Republicanism

Civic Republicanism is a political theory about freedom. The premises and aspirations of this political theory are perfectly captured by Iseult Honohan: 'Civic republicanism addresses the problem of freedom among human beings who are necessarily interdependent.'[2] The reference to interdependence is crucial and illuminating. Interdependence is not a sign of weakness or ineptitude, but a reminder that human beings are social beings, or as Cicero said: 'The primary reason for the public coming together is not so much weakness as a sort of innate desire on the part of human beings to form communities.'[3] To embrace interdependence is to recognize that social cooperation is not a choice but a natural necessity, and politics is the art of pooling resources and working as a team in order to maximize the benefits of social cooperation, while finding a just and equitable distribution for its costs.

According to Iseult Honohan, 'republican politics is concerned with enabling interdependent citizens to deliberate on, and realise, the common good.'[4] She is right to emphasize the dual aspects of 'deliberation' and 'common good' as distinctive features of republicanism, two areas where this tradition can be distinguished from liberalism.

As the name suggests, liberalism is primarily about liberty (or freedom), but liberalism gives a very specific interpretation of the meaning, and value, of freedom. Fundamentally liberalism accords pride of place in the scale of moral values to the individual, and hence individual freedom.[5] The individualistic postulation on which liberalism grounds its moral force finds validation in the idea of rights. From the *Déclaration des Droits de l'Homme et du Citoyen* in France in 1789, to the Universal Declaration of Human Rights in 1948, and its many elaborations in human rights law since then, there are many reasons to be grateful to liberalism. But there is a dark side to liberalism and human rights, as many scholars from many different and progressive traditions have pointed out over the centuries, including Jeremy Bentham (utilitarianism), Karl Marx (socialism), Mary Wollstonecraft (feminism) in the nineteenth century, and more recently Onora O'Neill.[6]

Under liberalism we don't just have the right to pursue our conceptions of the good as we see fit, but we also have the right to be self-seeking and self-centred, or even greedy and callous. This liberal conception of freedom justifies the right to bear arms in America, and the right not to wear a face mask during a pandemic. In its most extreme spin-off, which goes by the name of neo-liberalism, the rights accorded to us demand that the state is replaced by the market, the polis by market forces. According to neo-liberalism, competition (and not cooperation) becomes the only legitimate organizing principle for human activity. Neo-liberalism dismisses social justice as a mirage, it perceives the state as nothing more than a constant threat, or at best a necessary evil.[7]

Civic Republicanism is not dismissive of the concept of individual rights. It does not deny the importance of promoting individual interests or protecting individual rights. But at the same time the republican tradition wants to hold on to the belief that there is more to a democracy than the entitlement to exploit and be exploited, or the prerogative to prioritize private interests above the common good, or even the privilege for a single individual to prosper at the expense of the many who struggle and suffer. The idea of the 'common good' is notoriously difficult to define, and prone to abuse, but intuitively its appeal remains resolute and unyielding. It is a forceful reminder that, as we said before, no individual is self-sufficient, everyone needs others to prosper, and freedom is a social good and not a solipsistic paradigm.[8] Ultimately, emphasizing our duty towards the common good sets Civic Republicanism apart from liberal and libertarian theories centred on individual rights.

Republican citizenship

Civic Republicanism also firmly believes that freedom cannot be defined merely in terms of the absence of coercion or impediments to self-seeking individual desires and wishes (negative freedom), instead true freedom can only be realized through membership of a political community. The Roman Republic had an innovative way of defining the rights and duties of membership in a political community: citizenship. In ancient times enjoying the rights of citizenship was the main difference between the life of freedom in a Republic as opposed to life of subjugation under a monarchy.

In a monarchy there is a sovereign ruling over his or her 'subjects', whereas in a republic people are 'citizens'. As the term indicates, to be a 'subject' indicates subordination to the sovereign: subjects are under the complete and total control of the sovereign, they do not have a say in how they are governed, and they certainly don't have inalienable rights and freedoms. Citizens on the other hand have all the freedoms and benefits denied to subjects.

Romans turned their back on monarchy in 509 BC after the scandalous and capricious reign of Rome's seventh and last king Lucius Tarquinius Superbus, the final straw being the rape of Lucretia by Sextus Tarquinius, the king's son, which precipitated her suicide. The legendary story of Lucretia is immortalized in the paintings by Titian in 1571, Artemisia Gentileschi in 1627 and Rembrandt in 1664. The story of Lucretia did more harm to women throughout history than one can possibly imagine: the exaltation of the innocent victim's shame, the moral integrity of chastity (*pudicitia*) in contrast to the evil of lust (*libido*), and female virtue being identified with being a dutiful wife to her husband or father, making life impossible for women for centuries to come. In her 2019 Gifford Lecture, Mary Beard is keen to stress how the story of Lucretia relates to our own time: 'many of the standard templates we have for defining sexual violence, for excusing it, for giving alibis for it, for challenging women's accounts and motivations, are rooted in classical antiquity and in all the debates that classical antiquity has sparked in the literature and painting of the millennia that followed'. Beard encourages us to 'challenge some of the ways we have come to "think Lucretia" in our own day and age'.[9]

In their search for an alternative to monarchy, the Romans reinvented the concept of *politeia*, first used in Ancient Greece, which translates as 'constitution', originally meaning 'condition of citizenship', suggesting that the relationship between constitution and citizenship is extremely close.[10] Citizens enjoy equality, and through the idea of citizenship we come to grasp the key notion underpinning democracy that not just freedom but also equality is the essence of politics. In fact, as Cicero rightly points out in his text *On the Republic*: 'Nothing can be sweeter than liberty. Yet if it isn't equal throughout, it isn't liberty at all'.[11]

We said before that the Republican conception of politics wants to facilitate interdependent, equal citizens to cooperate and realize the common good. Civic Republicanism is essentially a set of institutions that enables citizens to shape their collective destiny through political participation, deliberation and collective decision making, and citizenship is at the heart of it. Of course, citizenship is also part of the liberal political landscape, but as we will see in Chapter 6 while liberal constitutions are legal systems committed to respecting and protecting individual rights, especially the right to property, republicanism accentuates a citizen's duties, a topic we already encountered in the previous chapter on Cicero's *On Duties*.

There is, however, an enduring puzzle about citizenship: if citizenship is a form of 'membership', then there is a permanent tension between those who are 'inside' a given polis, and those who are 'outside'. In other words, citizenship is defined by the dichotomy inclusion/exclusion. Furthermore, the concept of citizenship can aspire to be simultaneously universalistic and particularistic: liberal citizenship tends towards universalization, being expandable (in theory) to an almost infinite group of persons irrespective of social, ethnic, gender, or even territorial differences, whereas republican citizenship reinforces a citizen's capability to identify with a particular way of life that shapes one's political community.[12] It has been suggested that this tension between the universalizable (liberal) dimensions of citizenship and the particularistic (republican) dimensions of citizenship can be traced back to the transition in Rome from Republic to Empire.[13]

Perhaps of all the different aspects and virtues of citizenship, the most important one remains a citizen's ability to participate in politics. The capacity of all individuals to recognize their responsibilities in political rule, processes, decisions, and especially shared duties, is one of the most powerful and lasting contributions of Civic Republicanism to political philosophy. And it is also what Cicero found most appealing about the Roman Republic, and why he was prepared to die to defend it: Cicero saw in the participatory aspect of the Roman Republic the best antidote to the inequitable leadership of would-be dictators.

Domination and arbitrariness

One thing that Liberalism and Civic Republicanism have in common is the fact that both political theories are centred on the idea of freedom: what it is, why it is valued and how to protect it and make it flourish. But that's where similarities end. Republicanism has a very specific understanding of freedom, which superficially may seem to be very similar to the liberal conception, but in fact is very distinct and therefore fundamentally different.

In a liberal society our freedom is measured in terms of how far one can pursue one's own ends before one's actions are encroached upon and restricted by others.[14] In its purest form, freedom is defined in purely negative terms, and is perfectly captured by the libertarian philosopher Hillel Steiner's claim that an individual is unfree if, and only if, his or her doing of any action is rendered impossible by the action of another individual.[15] Republicanism has a different take on freedom: quite simply, freedom is the absence of domination.

The liberal idea of freedom as non-interference or non-coercion, and the republican idea of freedom as non-domination, may seem indistinguishable, but as often the case with philosophy the devil is in the detail. Civic Republicanism has a very technical understanding of domination, whereby domination is not just any interference, but specifically *arbitrary* interference, which means that an individual is unfree if, and only if, they are under the subjection and dependency of others.

One finds the conceptual roots of this idea of freedom as 'non-domination' in the Roman Republic. The etymology of the word 'domination' comes from the Latin word for house or dwelling, *domus*, the place where slaves (but also women and children) lived under the rule of a *dominus*, a lord or master, who enjoyed *dominatio* over them.[16] That domination starts at home is not a coincidence, as feminism has been telling us for many centuries. In Ancient Rome, law and custom vested (almost) absolute authority in the father, thus the *paterfamilias* enjoyed *patriapotestas*, which gave the father powers of life and death over the members of his family: legally a woman did not exist in her own right, and a newborn child was laid at the father's feet by the hearth, to be picked up by the father in token of acceptance to live and be reared, or not as the case may be.[17] However, close analysis of Roman law suggests a slightly less strict interpretation of Roman customs around marriage.[18]

In a monarchy, subjects are under the domination of their sovereign, who can wield arbitrary power over them, whereas in a republic citizens are not under the domination of anyone, not even their rulers. This was the revolutionary idea behind Roman citizenship, and why *Civis Romanus Sum* ('I am a Roman citizen'), a phrase allegedly coined by Cicero, was one of the most powerful slogans in Ancient Rome. Cicero used the phrase *Civis Romanus Sum* in a series of speeches he delivered in 70 BC against Gaius Verres, during the corruption and extortion trial of the former governor of Sicily, but we cannot know for certain whether that was the first time the term *Civis Romanus Sum* was used.[19]

A key concept in the republican definition of freedom as non-domination is 'arbitrariness'. There are two ways of thinking about arbitrariness. First, something can be said to be arbitrary if it is random, unpredictable, accidental. The roll of a dice is arbitrary. The other meaning of arbitrariness is capriciousness, whimsicality, or unprincipled behaviour. It is this conception of arbitrariness that republicanism has in mind when it alerts us to the dangers of arbitrary domination.

The Latin word *arbitrium* captures the discretionary power of someone who is in a position to make a decision or pass judgment, to choose or not to choose, at their pleasure. As Philip Pettit explains, an interference is arbitrary 'if it is subject just to the arbitrium, the decision or judgment, of the agent [who interferes]; the agent was in a position to choose it or not choose it, at their pleasure'.[20]

In our modern liberal democracy, while our rights and freedom are fully recognized, many people still live under the arbitrary domination of others. The working conditions of millions of people around the globe, including in liberal democracies, make claims of freedom and economic justice farcical. In Qatar, one of the richest countries in the world, the many thousands of migrant workers employed to build the stadiums for the 2022 FIFA World Cup allegedly worked eight hours a day, six days a week, for under £35 per week, or £5 per day. Things are not better in the West, contrary to what one might assume, where the exploitative, precarious nature of zero-hours contracts suggests that for many workers the social relations between employers and employees are akin to that of master–subject. We will return to some of these issues later, but first we need to show how Cicero had anticipated some of these risks, hence how his republican outlook can still be an inspiration to us today.

Domination in Ancient Rome

Arbitrary domination was the order of the day in Ancient Rome, even under the Roman Republic, and Cicero was aware of its threat to single individuals or to the polis more generally. Rome's domination over Italy, Europe and parts of North Africa and Asia was the result of a lethal military machine, famed for its discipline and engineering prowess. The discipline of its legions is legendary, but it came at a price, and arbitrariness played a role in it. Lack of discipline was not tolerated, and acts of cowardice, mutiny, desertion and insubordination were punished by the practice of decimation. The term 'decimation' comes from the Latin *decem* meaning ten, since in totally arbitrary fashion every tenth man in a group was executed by his cohorts, whether he was innocent or guilty: a legion of approximately 500 soldiers was divided into groups of ten, and each group would be forced to draw lots. The chosen soldier was then executed by his nine comrades, often by stoning or clubbing. Rome's civilization was built on violence.

Arbitrariness was also a cornerstone of Caesarism. Julius Caesar is often admired for his mercy, clemency and generosity. In war, when he captured enemy troops, he would let the leaders go free while enrolling the soldiers in his army – or turning them into slaves. He also famously spared Cicero's life after the civil war against Pompey, a decision that Cicero referred to as *insidiosa clementia*, or 'treacherous clemency'. The problem with Caesar's clemency is that it was a symptom of tyranny rather than virtue.[21] In *On the Republic*, Cicero reminds us that the reason monarchy is undesirable is that 'the property of the public (which is, as I said, the definition of the republic) was managed by one man's nod and wish'.[22]

To fully appreciate the arbitrary, tyrannical nature of clemency it may be instructive to think of a much-loved modern-day tradition like Thanksgiving. Traditionally the president of the United States kicks off the Thanksgiving holiday period by pardoning a turkey that will not be slaughtered with the other estimated 46 million turkeys killed each year for the sake of a family dinner. That single act of pardoning should not be confused with virtue, and Caesar was merely doing to human beings what the President of the United States does to one lucky turkey today. Lily Ross Taylor is probably right when she dismisses Caesar's policy of mercy as shrewd propaganda.[23]

Arbitrariness was also the defining feature in the practice of proscription, which was a decree of condemnation to death or banishment by declared enemies of the state, including confiscation of their property. The terror and brutality of the proscriptions were unprecedented. The heads of those killed were displayed in the Forum, for the public to see, and take note of. The fact that the proscription list was not fixed, and citizens could petition for names to be added or removed, contributed to the general state of fear. This was State terrorism at its most gruesome and indiscriminate stratum. There is a lot of truth in Richard Alson's claim that 'there was a terroristic element to this violence, scaring any who might think of opposing the regime'.[24]

There were two major proscriptions in Roman history. The first was in 82 BC, when Cicero was twenty-four years old, during the short-lived reign of dictator Lucius Cornelius Sulla. After securing unlimited power he took revenge on his enemies by offering a reward to anyone who would execute and bring back to Rome the heads of about 520 alleged enemies of the state, but in reality personal enemies, since he now identified with the state. The proscription of 82 BC was inevitably marred by acts of corruption. The proscription list was overseen by Sulla's freedman steward Lucius Cornelius Chrysogonus, who took the opportunity to enrich himself by convincing Sulla to include on the list of proscribed men those who were rich and with considerable private property. Since their properties would be confiscated, and their children and grandchildren would also lose any rights, proscriptions turned into legitimized theft.

The fact that Cicero's political career took off in the wake of Sulla's proscriptions is not insignificant: in 80 BC Cicero defended Sextus Roscius Amerinus, who was wrongly accused of patricide by Sulla. At the request of Chrysogonus, Roscius's father had been put on the proscription list, his only crime being that he was rich, and people envied his beautiful houses. After confiscating his property, Chrysogonus himself bought Roscius's family estates, valued at over 6 million sesterces, for a mere 2,000 sesterces. Sextus Roscius was accused of patricide as a smokescreen for the murderous, corrupt dealing that followed the proscription, and in the climate of mass terror that engulfed Rome during the proscriptions he could not find anyone prepared to plea for his innocence and defend him in a court of law. Except for the young Cicero, still only in his mid-20s, who bravely took on the case, his first litigation case. During the trial, Cicero took the bold decision to publicly accuse Chrysogonus of corruption. This was a career-defining moment for Cicero. Defending Sextus Roscius was a high-risk, almost reckless decision by Cicero, but Cicero successfully defended Sextus Roscius, winning the case against Chrysogonus. Cicero's legal dexterity was widely acclaimed. In the aftermath of the trial Cicero was the name on everyone's lips, and his political career took off in the most spectacular fashion.[25] But as a precaution, not knowing how Sulla was going to react to his unexpected success, as soon as the trial was over Cicero left Rome, for two years, taking this opportunity to tour Greece and improve his philosophy and rhetorical skills.

The second major proscription took place in 43 BC at the wishes of the second triumvirate of Octavian Caesar, Marc Antony and Marcus Lepidus. This time 2,000 people were on the list, and Cicero was one of them. He was executed near his home of Formia, roughly halfway between Rome and Naples, on 7 December 43 BC. His head and hands were cut off, as was the custom, for public display in the Forum. As the story goes, before his decapitated head was put on display on the Rostra, the public space facing the Senate where Cicero for many years had delivered his most famous orations, it was taken to Fulvia, the wife of Marc Antony, who stabbed Cicero's tongue with a golden hairpin. This was an act of vengeance for Cicero's extravagant character assassination of her husband in a series of famous speeches known as the *Philippics*. Furthermore, Fulvia's first husband was none other than Cicero's archenemy Publius Clodius Pulcher, with whom she had a daughter, Claudia, who subsequently became the wife of Octavian. Marc Antony was Fulvia's third husband. The proscriptions of 43 BC marked not only the death of Cicero but of the Roman Republic.

Cicero's 'res publica'

It was perhaps because of his personal experience with the arbitrary nature of domination that Cicero, in his text *On the Republic*, written in 51 BC, champions a republican framework. The text we have today is made up of fragments from different manuscripts and snippets of quotes in works by other authors over many centuries, which make up less than one-third of the original treatise, the rest is lost.

On the Republic is best known for Cicero's defence of the mixed constitution. *Per se*, this is not very original. Cicero is directly influenced by the Greek historian Polybius (c. 200 to c. 118 BC), author of *The Histories*, where he praises the mixed constitution of the Roman Republic (a working balance between monarchy, aristocracy and democracy) as the primary reason behind the success and overwhelming power of Rome over the known world. Polybius was in turn influenced by a passing remark by Aristotle in the *Politics* where he states the best constitution is made up of all existing forms. Cicero follows Polybius in pointing out how each of the three forms of government, on their own, inevitably collapse into something undesirable: monarchy turns to tyranny, aristocracy to oligarchy, democracy to mob rule. However, when mixed in a constitutional framework, the virtues of the three systems are secured and complement each other. In what follows I'm not going to elaborate on Cicero's analysis of the mixed constitution.[26] Instead, I will focus on the references to arbitrariness in the text, and on Cicero's definition of *res publica*.

There are many references in the text to the risks of arbitrariness when power is at the discretion of someone else, whether it be one single person or a mob:

> Although Cyrus of Persia was an exceptionally just and wise monarch, that form of government was not, in my view the most desirable; for the property of the public (which is, as I said, the definition of the republic) was managed by one man's *nod and wish*.[27]

The supreme power exercised by the Athenian people was transformed into the mad and irresponsible *caprice* of the mob.[28]

But if, violently or otherwise, the populace deposes a just king, or if, as more frequently happens, it tastes the blood of the aristocracy and subjects the entire state to its wild *caprice*.[29]

Cicero strongly believed that the best and only way to protect the people from the arbitrary domination of others is to invest them with political authority. The term *res publica* literally means 'the public thing'. Cicero's understanding of 'the public' is in terms of 'the people', *res publica res populi*: the public affairs are the people's affairs. This formula clearly and succinctly indicates that for Cicero the people are both the primary concern of government and the source of authority; furthermore, government should always be in the people's common interest.[30] Cicero's apparently tautological statement *res publica res populi* in fact reveals an idea which is fundamental to the tradition of Civic Republicanism in political theory: the people as the essence of the State,[31] a guiding principle immortalized in the words 'We the People' in the Preamble to the Constitution of the United States (and of India).

The term *populi* (or *populus*) is tricky, to put it mildly. It refers to a juridic or constitutional entity, the citizen body of the Republic.[32] It is to be distinguished from the term *popularis*, which has a distinctive populist flavour, and as such is prone to a negative connotation. As a republican Cicero believed in the people, but he was suspicious of the political manipulation of the people at the hands of populist politicians, like Clodius or Julius Caesar, who put their own interests above the common good.

There are two aspects of Cicero's affinity between *res publica* and *res populi* worth emphasizing.[33] First, the imperative of political participation. For the people to take control of both their personal and public affairs, active citizenship is required. Of course, for Cicero active participation in public affairs should be motivated by the public good, not by private interests, and Cicero believed that knowledge of philosophy was a necessary precondition for nurturing the idea of the common good. This in part explains Cicero's phenomenal philosophical output. In Chapter 1, we saw how Cicero broke down the dichotomy between *otium* and *negotium* by hinting that he did not write philosophy for leisure or for his personal amusement, instead writing philosophy was for Cicero a contribution to political affairs.

The extent to which Cicero's philosophical writings were groundbreaking is often not appreciated enough, for no other reason than that he wrote his philosophy in Latin. At the time all philosophy was in Greek, and only in Greek, therefore only the privileged elite had access to it. Cicero single-handedly changed it by making philosophy accessible to the people of Rome by writing in their language. This proved to be more difficult than it may appear. Cicero had to invent a new vocabulary to translate Greek terms in a language that did not have the words to express philosophical concepts, and it is thanks to Cicero that a great deal of Greek philosophy has survived, and that philosophy prospered in the West. Cicero is often dismissed for being elitist and conservative, but this is inaccurate. He truly believed that *anyone* could be educated, and that everyone could learn philosophy. Philosophy was not the prerogative of kings but rightly belonged to everyone, to the common people: this belief is profoundly anti-elitist.

The second aspect of Cicero's claim that the public affairs (*res publica*) are the people's affairs (*res populi*) is the fact that Cicero's political philosophy is driven by a profound sense of equality. In fact, Cicero realized that the Latin language did not have the vocabulary he needed to express his thoughts. At the time there was a word for equity or fairness (*aequitas*), and one for equality as parity or sameness (*pari*), but not a word for equality distinct from parity. To fix this he coined a new term, *aequabilitas*, to capture the idea of equality as equilibrium.[34] It is interesting to note that in *De Natura Deorum* (On the Nature of the Gods), written in 45 BC, Cicero uses the term *aequabilitas* when referring to the regularity of the revolutions of the heavenly bodies, which suggests an equilibrium in the universe.[35]

Cicero's concern for equality comes out in many passages in his text *On the Republic*. I have mentioned before how for Cicero liberty, unless equal throughout, isn't liberty at all. In other passages Cicero praises the importance of equality and the risks of inequality. He tells us that a mixed constitution, which was his preferred form of government 'has, in the first place, a widespread element of equality which free men cannot long do without'.[36] He also explains that unless the people 'own' the republic, there is no republic, and that equal justice is the defining feature of a republic that is truly a republic: 'For what is a state other than an equal partnership in justice?'[37]

As for the risks to justice of a society defined by inequality, Cicero's words are as true today as they were in 51 BC: 'Money, name, and property, if divorced from good sense ... lapse into total degradation ... And indeed there is no more degenerate kind of state than that in which the richest are supposed to be the best'.[38] Sadly it appears that not a great deal has changed in the last 2,000 years. We will return to the issue of inequality in the Epilogue.

Conclusion

Cicero lived, and died, for an ideal: the Roman Republic. While imperfect, especially seen from the point of view of the twenty-first century, the Roman Republic still encapsulates the essence of Civic Republicanism, and Civic Republicanism offers an alternative theory of government to liberal democracy. At the core of the Civic Republican model we find the idea of creating the institutional arrangements that preserve individual freedom as non-domination.[39] Cicero highlighted the importance of equality in these institutional arrangements; he would be shocked, and alarmed, by the grotesque levels of domestic and global inequality in the modern world.

4

The value of friendship

*We do so many things for friends which
we would never do for ourselves.*

MARCUS TULLIUS CICERO (ON FRIENDSHIP)

Cicero famously said, *sine amicitia, vita esse nullam*. This translates as 'life without friends is simply not worth living', or more simply and economically, 'life is nothing without friendship'. The message is powerful and urgent, whatever the translation. It speaks to the essence of being human, to our most basic social needs, and aspirations. This suggests that friendship is an important topic, which in the past attracted much attention in philosophical circles, although regrettably that is no longer the case.[1]

Today the best place to look for a meaningful enquiry into friendship is fiction, *in primis* perhaps the remarkable four-volume saga by Elena Ferrante, *My Brilliant Friend*, which focuses on friendship between two Neapolitan women, or the popular novels by Irish writer Sally Rooney. Of course, friendship crops up in almost every novel we read, since friendship is the cement of the social world. Novels are an invaluable source of information on the human psyche, and a good starting point for philosophical explorations. For philosophers, friendship is a perfect topic given its many related concepts: truthfulness, trust, loyalty and love.

Cicero would approve of reading literature, and poetry, and engaging with all other art forms, as a way of gaining knowledge. In *Pro-Archia* (62 BC) he writes:

> Do you think it possible that we could find a supply for our daily speeches, when discussing such a variety of matters, unless we were to cultivate our minds by the study of literature? Or that our minds could bear being kept so constantly on the stretch if we did not relax them by that same study? But I confess that I am devoted to those studies, let others be ashamed of them if they have buried themselves in books without being able to produce anything out of them for the common advantage or anything which may bear the eyes of men and the light. But why need I be ashamed.[2]

The current tendency in many countries to cut down on investment in the humanities is dangerously short-sighted. Cicero was a Renaissance man, before the Renaissance.[3]

Like Aristotle before him, Cicero took a keen interest on the nature of friendship, and as is often the case with Cicero his analysis of friendship has clear political undertones: for Cicero, the personal is political. In what follows, starting with a brief overview of friendship in Plato and Aristotle, we will consider why we should value friendship at both a personal and civic level, and why tyranny undermines friendship. Finally, with the help of Cicero the sorry state of friendship in our modern, cyber-obsessed society will be considered.

Plato and Aristotle on friendship

Plato and Aristotle both struggled to come up with definitions of friendship, which is an indication of just how difficult it is to get a hold of this concept. Nevertheless, they present us with gems of insight, which Cicero refers to in his own analysis on friendship.

According to Plato, our best hope to make sense of friendship is via the concept of love, and Socrates famously suggests that we think of love as the desire for something that someone lacks.[4] The obvious objection with this definition of love is why we keep loving our beloved, since they are present in our lives. Plato's answer is that we have a desire to have the love of our beloved forever; that is, we desire not lacking them at some point in the future. That's not very convincing.

What is most interesting about this idea of love as the desire of what we lack is that it also speaks to the essence of philosophy. From *philein* meaning 'to love', and *sophia* meaning 'wisdom', philosophy is the love of wisdom, which suggests that we love wisdom precisely because we acknowledge our lack of wisdom. This is worth remembering: those who don't have time for philosophy are guilty of lack of modesty, since they wrongly assume that they already have all the knowledge and wisdom they need.

But if love is supposed to help us make sense of friendship, what exactly are we lacking when we seek friendship? Aristotle breaks down friendship into three parts: utility-based friendship, that we pursue for mutual benefit; pleasure-based friendship, which we pursue for mutual pleasure; virtue-based friendship, which we pursue for the sake of perfecting or augmenting our mutual virtues.[5]

This tripartite analysis doesn't add up to a definition of friendship, although there appears to be a common denominator across the three types of friendship singled out by Aristotle, namely, reciprocity: a person becomes a friend when, being loved, they love in return. The reciprocal force of love is perfectly captured by Dante in Canto V of the 'Inferno' in the *Divine Comedy*, in one of the most hauntingly beautiful lines of poetry ever written: *Amor, ch'a nullo amato amar perdona*, which translates as 'Love, which exempts no one who's loved from loving'.

Aristotle goes on to say that while utility-based friendships are sought by people in the latter stages of their lives, and pleasure-based friendships by people in their youth, true or perfect friendship occurs between people who are good and alike in virtue. This is the starting point of Cicero's own reflections on friendship.

Personal friendship

Cicero approaches the question 'what is friendship?' by way of another question: what is the *value* of friendship? Or perhaps more directly: why have friends? Understanding the *value* we put on friendship will tell us a great deal about what friendship is, and why it is important to us.

Cicero suggests that friendship brings considerable advantages, although he goes on to explain that one should not enter friendship for instrumental reasons, merely for the benefits that friendship brings. Cicero mentions three reasons why friendship is valuable: first, no life is worth living without the mutual love of friends; secondly, friendship shines the light of hope into the future; and thirdly, the fact that looking at a true friend is like seeing an image of yourself. The latter two reasons remain a bit opaque, in fact Cicero does not tell us what he means precisely when he says that friendship makes the future seem more hopeful, or how (and why) we tend to identify with our friends. Readers are of course free to speculate and philosophize on these claims, but for now it is best to concentrate on the first of the three reasons he gives, which is also, philosophically, the meatier of the three.

To help us understand why no life is worth living without the mutual love of friends, Cicero starts by asking a preliminary question: namely, why do people seek friendships? Cicero contemplates different possible answers. For example, perhaps because we are weak and helpless, and we hope to gain something from the reciprocal arrangements of friendship. This would suggest that friendship is a sign of weakness, since we pursue friendships to compensate for our failings or inadequacies, but Cicero refuses to accept this line of reasoning.[6] Friendship cannot be explained, or justified, on instrumental terms, merely because of the benefits it brings. Instead, Cicero wants to convince us that friendship has an intrinsic value: 'friendship … has its deep and true origin in nature, not weakness'.[7] What Cicero means by 'nature' here is love: 'friendship arises from nature rather than from need, from the inclination of the soul accompanied by a certain sentiment of love, rather than from calculation of a relationship's potential usefulness' and 'we don't seek friendship with an expectation of gain, but regard the feeling of love as its own reward'.[8]

This last quote is followed by a curious aside: 'It's no wonder that those who are interested only in pleasure (just like cattle!) disagree with what I say!'.[9] Exactly who is at the receiving end of Cicero's sharp, scathing remark? It could be sympathizers of rival philosophical schools of thought, like hedonists or epicureans, but I think Cicero always reserves his most cutting, harsh, critical language for his political foes. My hunch is that Cicero is probably referring to Marc Antony, the bestial qualities of the cattle being a strong hint here. In his *Philippics*, also known as *In Antonium* (Against Antony) which were also written in 44 BC, the same year as his treatise *On Friendship*, Cicero repeatedly scolds Marc Antony for his sexually-deprived antics, for example in the second *Philippic* Cicero writes:

> when, worn out with wine and fornication, you [Marc Antony] daily indulged, within that shameless house of yours, in every type of perversion.[10]

and follows it with this shortly later:

> You assumed the toga of manhood – and immediately turned it into a toga of womanhood [a prostitute's frock]. First you were a common prostitute [rent boy]: you had a fixed rate for your shameful services, and not a low one either. But soon Curio appeared on the scene. He saved you from having to support yourself as a prostitute, fitted you out in the dress of a married lady, as it were, and settled you in good, steady wedlock. No slave boy bought for sexual gratification was ever as much in his master's power as you were in Curio's. How many times did his father throw you out of the house! How many times did he post guards to stop you crossing the threshold! But you, with night to aid you, lust to drive you, and the prospect of payment to compel you,

had yourself lowered in through the roof-tiles. ... But let us now pass over his sexual crimes and depravity: there are some things I cannot decently relate.[11]

So now Fulvia's vengeful act of stabbing Cicero's tongue with her hairpin after he had been decapitated, mentioned at the end of Chapter 3, makes more sense, considering that she was Marc Antony's wife.

There is also another quote in Cicero's *On Friendship* that, in light of what he says about Marc Antony in the *Philippics*, could be a clue of who he had in mind when he wrote the following lines: 'There can be no friendship except among people who are good ... whose life and conduct display reliability, integrity, fairness and generosity, who avoid greed, *sensuality and reckless conduct, and do so consistently*.'[12]

Let's leave Cicero's animosity towards Marc Antony aside and get back to the philosophy of friendship. To force home the point that the value of friendship is intrinsic and not instrumental, Cicero introduces two thought experiments. In the first, he invites us to imagine that some deity granted us any and every natural desire we may have, but on the condition that we don't share the experience with any other human being. Would we accept this divine gift? Cicero's intuition is that we wouldn't, because any experience has value only to the extent that it can be shared with others. As Cicero says: 'Who would be so unfeeling as to put up with such a life? In isolation, who wouldn't lose enjoyment of all delights?'[13] In the second thought experiment, Cicero quotes the Ancient Greek philosopher Archytas of Tarentum, who died in 347 BC: 'If anyone ascends into the heavens and gazes out over the universe and the beauty of the constellations, the marvellous sight will scarcely appeal to him; but if he has someone to describe it to, then it's the most delightful thing of all!'[14] Cicero is right of course. Solitude is something we endure, not crave – unless you are Jean-Jacques Rousseau.[15] That is why, bar a few exceptional circumstances, people tend to seek company when going to the cinema, out for a meal, or to a concert or festival. What matters to us is not seeing a particular movie, eating at a particular restaurant, or listening to our favourite musicians live, but sharing the moment. Friendship adds colour to our otherwise black and white existence.

Civic friendship

In our modern lexicon the term 'friendship' usually refers to a personal endeavour. Individualism has colonized this term to the extent that today friendship is, by definition, understood to mean a personal relationship between two or more individuals. But that was not always the case. The Greek term *philia* is broader than the English 'friendship'. *Philia* also includes the relations between husband and wife, parents and children, siblings, and crucially even fellow citizens.

Aristotle said that to *philein* towards someone is to wish for them what you believe to be good things, not for your own sake but for theirs, and being inclined, so far as you can, to make those good things happen. Cicero agrees with Aristotle, and goes on to tell us that the Latin for friendship, *amicitia*, is derived from *amor*, meaning love: 'Isn't love (from which our word for friendship is derived) the real force behind the sharing of good will?'[16]

Of course, it has to be the right type of love. Cicero warns us that 'love of money is the greatest threat to friendship',[17] and he goes on to explain how material inequalities are the antithesis of friendship, and also a threat to political stability:

> Who on earth would wish to be showered with riches and to enjoy an abundance of every kind of possession if it meant not loving or being loved by another? Surely this is the life of tyrants: to be without trust, affection or reliable expectation of good will, always anxious and suspicious about everything, with no opportunity for friendship.[18]

This last quote is meaningful for two reasons. First, it picks up on the theme of trust. In Chapter 2 we saw that in *On Duties* Cicero told us that the foundation of justice is trust, and now he tells us that 'What secures the stability and constancy we seek in friendship is trust. Nothing is stable if it can't be trusted.'[19] Stability is clearly a political concept, thus we get a real sense that for Cicero friendship is not just personal but also political, perhaps a civic duty, certainly part of what citizenship requires and stands for.[20]

Secondly, the reference to 'the life of tyrants' allows Cicero to introduce the issue of equality, a recurring preoccupation in Cicero's political outlook. Cicero uses the idea of friendship to admonish those with aspirations for glory and absolute power:

> For who could love the person he fears, or the person he thinks fears him? Tyrants may be treated to a pretence of affection, at least for a time, but once they run into trouble, as tends to happen, it becomes obvious how few friends they have.[21]

The important point here is that a polis dictated by a tyrant, where fear rules, will destroy the fabric of citizenship. Tyranny is the antithesis of equality and the enemy of friendship.

For Cicero it is not only a case that gross material inequalities undermine friendship and therefore citizenship, but also that true friendship must be grounded on social equality. Thus, Cicero tells us that 'it's especially important to treat friends of lower rank as equals',[22] and that 'those of higher rank who are bound by friendship or other close connection should make themselves equal to their inferiors, and those of lower rank should not be hurt if a friend surpasses them in talent, luck or rank'.[23] For someone often dismissed for his conservative and elitist leaning, these statements shine a whole new light on Cicero's political philosophy. As a true republican, Cicero was more egalitarian than he is given credit for.[24]

Friendship in times of tyranny

When Brutus, Cassius and his associates stabbed Julius Caesar twenty-three times on the Ides of March of 44 BC, they expected the news to be received with jubilation and euphoria. This historical moment was supposed to mark the re-birth of the Roman Republic, symbolically comparable to the end of the monarchy in 509 BC when the seventh king of Rome Lucius Tarquinius Superbus was overthrown in a revolt led by Lucius Junius Brutus, a distant relative of Brutus himself. This was not to be the case. The death of Julius Caesar had the opposite impact of what his assassins hoped: they considered themselves as liberators, but the people of Rome saw them as aspiring tyrants.

One of the reasons why the people of Rome did not trust Brutus has a lot to do with friendship. Brutus and Julius Caesar were close friends. As young men they grew up in the same intellectual circles, and later Julius Caesar had proved his friendship towards Brutus and his other assassins when he pardoned them for siding with Pompey against him in the civil war. To the eyes of the people of Rome, Brutus and the others had betrayed Caesar's friendship.[25] In Roman times, friendship was a powerful ethical concept, a mark of virtue. To act against a friend was deplorable, inexcusable, unpardonable. It is not a coincidence that 'friends' is the first word in Marc Antony's beautiful oration in Shakespeare's play *Julius Caesar*.

In the immediate aftermath of the assassination, Brutus raised his dagger, still dripping with Caesar's blood, turned to the people of Rome in the Forum, and shouted: 'Cicero! Cicero!'. No one was more shocked by this turn of events than Cicero himself, since he had been kept in the dark about the conspiracy to kill Julius Caesar. We will never know whether that was because they didn't trust him, or because they thought he was too squeamish and incapable of violent murder. Whatever the reason, Cicero was not involved at any stage in Julius Caesar's murder, but after Brutus's blood-drenched theatrics the whole of Rome probably thought that he was the mastermind behind the assassination.

This may have been the principal reason behind Cicero's decision to write a philosophical treatise on friendship in the early fall of 44 BC, a few months after Julius Caesar's assassination. He had written about the ethics of friendship before, in particular in *De Finibus* (On Moral Ends), finished in 45 BC, but he now felt the need to devote a whole treatise on the topic. Cicero is keen to stress that friendship is not an absolute virtue, instead there are limits to our obligations of friendship. Here Cicero is making a political statement: friendship is important for one's well-being, even essential, but the Republic always comes first. Our political obligation to justice trumps our moral obligation to our friends. The bond that ties us together in a republic is a bond of friendship, even with strangers. We should care and love the republic, perhaps even more so than the care and love we feel for our friends. Cicero's *On Friendship* is a remarkable piece of work, where philosophical analysis is driven by emotional verve and political commitment.[26]

In the last analysis, Julius Caesar was a tyrant, an enemy of the Roman Republic, and tyrants cannot have any friends at all. Julius Caesar was not a friend of the Roman Republic, or of the Roman people. That's why for Cicero the actions of Brutus and the other assassins were not an affront to friendship. Cicero refused to accept that appeals to friendship can justify dishonesty or dishonourable conduct, an important principle we would do well to remember. Judith Shklar, one of the few contemporary political theorists to engage with Cicero's views on the subject of friendship, sums it up perfectly: 'To act with one's friend for the republic is perfection. To prefer him to the republic is absolutely wrong.'[27]

Conclusion: On cyber friendship

Our highly individualistic, inegalitarian society is not conducive to friendship, at least not the right kind of friendship. Utility-based and pleasure-based friendships abound, but not virtue-based friendships. And yet, technology has apparently made it very easy to have hundreds if not thousands of friends. According to one study, from 2008, Facebook users on average have 281 friends.[28] One wonders what Cicero would say about cyber-friendships.

Because he was an accomplished letter writer, Philip Freeman thinks that Cicero would approve of Facebook in general, and also potentially of the friendships one makes on social media. Freeman goes on to specify that Cicero's love of Facebook would not be unconditional: 'But I think Cicero would draw an important distinction between posting photos of his cat to thousands of followers and intimate interactions with his closest friends, whether written or face-to-face. Cicero would probably say that the social media universe can be a good thing if used properly and terribly harmful to the soul if not.'[29] I'm not convinced. First of all, social media platforms like Facebook are not conducive to the search for truth, in fact they are very much search engines for post-truth, often generating great quantities of damaging fake news. As we saw in Chapter 2, Cicero argues that we have a duty to truth, and social media platforms get in the way of that. Secondly, the so-called friendships one accumulates on social platforms are at best instrumental, and at worse demoralizing and destructive. They are instrumental in the sense that people are more interested in the number of friends they have on Facebook or Twitter or Instagram or TikTok than the quality of friends. A person's social capital, and influence, can conveniently be measured in terms of the number of followers they have on social media, and of course under capitalism 'influence' has a monetary value. But cyber-friendships can also be demoralizing since our virtual friends are not there when we need them most: the experience one shares with a friend, in flesh and blood, is on a different scale, or *qualia*, from any pre-recorded exchange on a screen. One can have a thousand cyber-friends and still experience the most devastating loneliness.

There is growing evidence that Instagram (owned by Facebook) is toxic to young people, especially younger girls, being linked to increases in the rate of anxiety and depression. There is also a concern that Facebook is not doing enough to stem the tide of fake news, allowing the forces of post-truth and misinformation to cause unimaginable social harm by tearing a hole in the fabric of factuality. Under the flag of freedom of speech Facebook is profiting from a nasty and brutish unregulated forum, where people feel it is their fundamental right to abuse others.[30] And yet, we are told that the future is 'metaverse'. Sadly, 'metaverse' is not where philosophy (metaphysics) meets poetry (verse), instead in the words of Facebook's founder and CEO Mark Zuckerberg metaverse is the 'convergence of physical, augmented, and virtual reality in a shared online space'.[31] This is terrifying: Zoom on steroids, with a touch of magic mushrooms.

The selling point of metaverse is that it is bigger and better virtual 'reality', where we can have more thrilling interactions with our many 'friends' on social media platforms. This is precisely what is most disconcerting. Whatever the benefits of metaverse, let's not kid ourselves: it has very little to do with reality, and even less to do with friendship. There are very few virtues in Facebook's virtual reality.

Back in 1974, many years before the internet was invented, and ten years before Zuckerberg was even born, Harvard philosopher Robert Nozick came up with the thought experiment known as 'the experience machine': suppose a machine was invented that would give you any experience you desired, by stimulating your brain so that you would think and feel you were writing a great novel, or making a friend, or reading an interesting book. All the time you would be floating in a tank, with electrodes attached to your brain. Should you plug into this machine for life, pre-programming your life experiences? Nozick argued that it would be foolish to plug in, because living life through the experience machine would remove any meaning from our lives. He was right, of course.[32]

Zuckerberg's metaverse is not 'reality', and the people we interact with on social media are not our 'friends'. Cicero would be appalled by the idea that what makes life worth living is having access to a more augmented virtual reality inhabited by virtual friends. If Cicero were living today, he would probably change his most famous statement about friendship to something along the lines of: 'life without friends is simply not worth living, but life with *only* cyber-friends is also not worth living'.

5

Getting old, with *decorum*

To be ignorant of what occurred before you
were born is to remain always a child.
MARCUS TULLIUS CICERO (ORATOR AD M. BRUTUM)

We live in an ageing society. The global population aged sixty years or over numbered 962 million in 2017, more than twice as large as in 1980 when there were 382 million older persons worldwide. The number of older persons is expected to double again by 2050, when it is projected to reach nearly 2.1 billion. In 2030, they are expected to outnumber children under the age of ten (1.41 billion versus 1.35 billion); in 2050, projections indicate that there will be more people over sixty than adolescents and young adults between the ages of ten and twenty-four (2.1 billion versus 2.0 billion). Globally, the number of persons aged eighty years or over is projected to increase more than threefold between 2017 and 2050, rising from 137 million to 425 million.[1]

The good news is that these statistics reflect our increasing standards of living, in fact while today two-thirds of the world's older persons live in the developing regions, by 2050 it is expected that nearly eight in ten of the world's older persons will be living in developed regions. The bad news is that modern society tends to see people in old age as a burden, a wasteful drain on resources, a social encumbrance. We may agree, theoretically, that a just society ought to show concern and respect for its more senior citizens, but of course we disagree on precisely what form this should take, and anyway what we practice is not always what we preach. During the first wave of the Covid-19 pandemic in 2020, modern society forgot all about the concern and respect for the elderly.[2]

The philosophy of old age

'Old age' is a notoriously nebulous concept, very hard to define. Small children think that anyone over thirty is 'old', and even as adults we struggle to draw a line where mid-life ends, and 'old age' begins. What cannot be denied is that, at least in contemporary Western society, 'old' has many pejorative connotations, which reflects the pervasive unconscious bias of ageism: the prejudice, stigmatization, negative discrimination and even oppression aimed at a particular person or group of people because of their age.[3]

One of the problems we face today is that society fails to appreciate that being an old person is still being a person. Behind common views on old age there is a particular notion of personhood. To think of old age as the culmination of a life, as the last stage before death, when the games are done, nothing more lies ahead, with nothing more to live for but wait for the inevitable, is to fail to appreciate a fundamental aspect of being a person: that whatever one's age, or circumstances, one never ceases to experience life. Those experiences may be more restricted and laboured than they once were, but they are still there, the essence of our phenomenological existence.

This is sometimes referred to as the *seriatum* theory of the self. 'Seriatum' is Latin for 'in a series', meaning that a person is not identifiable with a single, overarching life plan, or quest, or project, that gives meaning to our existence. On the contrary, the 'seriatim self' values each relationship and experience intrinsically, since every stage of one's life, including old age, is valued for 'in-the-present activities and relationships'.[4]

Be that as it may, there is an obsession with wanting to identify precisely when 'old age' begins. One popular suggestion is that 'old age' starts when people reach the age of retirement, which is roughly around the age of sixty-five, allowing for national variations. The dividing line is drawn where paid work ends and pension payments begin. The problem with this approach is that it assumes that after a certain age a person is deemed to be no longer productive, therefore no longer able to make a meaningful contribution to society. This is both inaccurate and meanspirited. As we will see, Cicero would have a problem with this portrayal of old age, and rightly so.

Modern views on old age

The received view is that people in old age are due extra care from society, including extra resources, as a matter of justice. There are two reasons why in old age we should expect more from a just society.

First, because a just society should look after the least advantaged members of our society, and old age qualifies us as 'least advantaged' by virtue of the fact that we enter the phase of our life when we are more vulnerable, more weak, more ill, less autonomous, and so on. The second reason why in old age we should expect more from a just society is due to a sense of justice as reciprocity: it is only fair that those who have given to society in the productive part of their lives should now receive back from society in the subsequent, less productive stage of their lives. It is on the basis of these two views that most people accept that 'senior' members of our society are entitled to a special set of rights. As we enter the most vulnerable phase of our life, those in old age have a right to live with dignity, which in the final chapters of our lives tends to be eroded by poverty, ill health and inadequate (and expensive) health care.[5] It has even been suggested that people in old age have unique *human* rights.

The received view on old age makes sense, and it appears to be harmless, but maybe that's not the case. We know that the way to hell is paved with good intentions; the same is true of social injustice. The extra layer of anxiety and apprehension we project to people in old age is well intended of course, but it may also do a disservice to the people it wants to benefit. It is hard to read about 'old age' as a special concern without thinking of offensive judgements about a group of people who are 'over the hill' or 'past the sell-by date' or 'the have-beens' or 'those with one foot in the grave' or 'dotty old senile' or 'old age brigade'. We want to help them because, deep down, we pity them. By embracing this attitude, we risk doing a great injustice to those who live in old age. To avoid making this mistake, a radical, new approach is required, one that is respectful and not condescending towards old age. There is no better place to look for inspiration than to revisit the philosophical work by Cicero on 'Old Age'.

In *On Old Age* (44 BC), Cicero writes: 'To be respected is the crowning glory of old age.'[6] To be respected. The way we think of old age has the potential risk of undermining the respect people in old age deserve. The period of old age is at times even compared to the period of infancy in our lives: both defined by vulnerability and frailty, both requiring our care and attention. But this comparison is profoundly disrespectful, indeed as Cicero reminds us: 'So old age, you see, far from being sluggish and feeble, is really very lively, and perpetually active, and still busy with the pursuit of earlier years. Some people never stop learning, however old they are.'[7]

Cicero on old age

Cicero's text is one of the earliest philosophical investigations on old age. Here Cicero defends the counter-intuitive view that old age is arguably the best part of one's life, therefore refuting the generally held prejudice against people in old age as weak, vulnerable, incapable of making meaningful contributions, and thus a mere burden to society.

Cicero considers, and refutes, four standard reasons why old age is said to be bad. First, it is said that old age is bad because it makes us unproductive (in Cicero's terms, it 'withdraws us from active pursuits'). Cicero refutes this assumption on the grounds that in old age we may not be as physically strong as in our youth, but we are wiser, and that is infinitely more important: 'great deeds are not done by strength or speed or physique: they are the products of thought, and character, and judgment. And far from diminishing, such qualities actually increase with age.'[8]

Second, it is said that old age is bad because in old age we are physically weaker. Again, Cicero thinks this is absurd. Of course it is true that one is physically stronger in youth, but physical strength is less important than intellectual agility, which improves with age: 'Every stage of life has its own characteristics: boys are feeble, youths in their prime are aggressive, middle-aged men are dignified, old people are mature.'[9]

Third, it is said that old age deprives us of almost all sexual pleasures. Cicero thinks that this is nonsense. First of all because contrary to what people think, people in old age still have sexual desires and are sexually active. But even if old age were to flatten our libido, according to Cicero this is only to be welcomed, since old age gives us freedom from a type of slavery: 'I have known many old men who had no complaints about their age or its *liberating* release from physical pleasure.'[10] Why liberating? Because in youth reason is, and always will be, the slave of sexual passions: 'We ought to feel very grateful to old age for removing the desire to do what is wrong. For such feelings cloud a man's judgment, obstruct his reasoning capacity, and blind his intelligence: let sensuality be present, and a good life becomes impossible.'[11] A similar position is defended by Seneca in his essay *On Old Age*: 'Perhaps not wanting any is a surrogate for pleasure. How sweet it is to have outworn desires and left them behind!'.[12]

Fourth, it is said that old age is bad because old age is not far removed from death. Cicero thinks that this is a non-starter: following in the footsteps of Epicurean philosopher Lucretius, Cicero reminds us that death is not something we should fear: 'There are two alternatives: either death completely destroys human souls, in which case it is negligible; or it removes the soul to some place of eternal life – in which case its coming is greatly to be desired. There can be no third possibility.'[13] Here Cicero is echoing Epicurus's famous statement: death is nothing to us, seeing that, when we are, death is not come, and when death has come, we are not.

Having refuted four standard arguments why old age is bad, Cicero goes on to argue that old age is to be welcomed, not scorned: it is in old age that we are most productive intellectually, which is the most valuable type of work. The problem is that society fails to recognize the contribution that people can still make in old age, and this is a great injustice.

Admittedly, Cicero's ode to old age is problematic on many levels, prompting Norberto Bobbio to write that he finds this eulogistic genre nauseating.[14] One problem is the fact that what Cicero referred to as 'old age' is very different from what today we consider to be old age, given the changes in life expectancy, at least in rich, industrialized nations. Also, Cicero was writing for a class of people who would naturally have many slaves to look after them in old age, which is very convenient; we can only speculate how Cicero would have felt about coping with the many physical and mental challenges of old age without slaves to look after him.

And yet, there are many aspects of Cicero's analysis that are still as valid today as they were 2,000 years ago, which is why re-reading Cicero can help us make sense of the relationship between old age, inequality and justice.

His analysis resists the condescending and patronizing view society tends to have of the elderly. Cicero reminds us that we should not pity people for being old, instead we should recognize the fact that people in old age still have a great deal to offer to society. Cicero truly believes that old age does not make us useless, or worthless, and perhaps the problem with our modern society is that it has ceased to see its senior citizens as citizens, instead it considers them as a burden, both financially and morally. Just another tax that we must pay, or another duty that we must fulfil.

One possible counter-argument to Cicero's rosier picture about old age is that during his time people did not live as long as they do now, therefore by the age of sixty, one was deemed 'old' only because a person was close to the age when most people tended to die of natural causes. Today we live on average much longer. The threshold of old age has shifted by about twenty years, so much so that human life, traditionally divided into three stages, has been extended to the so-called 'fourth age'. If we want to improve the conditions of people living in 'old age', we could start by using this term only for people over eighty years of age, and use another term, the 'age of *decorum*' perhaps, for the category of sixty-five to eighty. Nevertheless, reading Cicero on old age is important, and necessary, precisely because he goes against the grain: it makes old age (whenever that is) dignified, empowering and almost desirable.

A republican view of old age

Cicero's treatise on old age is important also for another reason: it hints to a political alternative to a rights-based approach. Cicero did not write a book on rights, but as we know he wrote a book on our obligations or duties, *De Officiis* (On Duties). It would be a mistake to jump to the conclusion that Cicero did not write about rights only because the concept of rights had not been invented yet. While it is true that the idea of rights was developing at the time, the Romans had a strong sense of citizenship, including the conception of the rights that comes with it. As was discussed in Chapter 3, the Roman phrase *Civis Romanus Sum* (I'm a Roman Citizen) captures all that is most noble about Roman civilization, and that includes a conception of rights attached to citizenship. During Cicero's life Rome was still a republic, and citizenship is a fundamental concept for any republic, but the way citizenship is defined in the republican tradition in political theory is in important ways different from the way citizenship is defined in the liberal tradition.

The liberal conception of citizenship puts a great deal of emphasis on the rights we enjoy as citizens. Not only the right to participate in the political affairs of our community, but also the justified claims we can make on others, starting from the state, by virtue of our rights to citizenship: the right to education, to health care, to housing, to legal representation, to a clean environment, perhaps even the right to a free internet, which may or may not be necessary to develop our friendships.[15] In the liberal tradition, rights are identified with entitlements, which means that a right gives us the entitlement to make demands on others, for our own benefit.[16]

On the other hand, the republican conception of citizenship is not just about our rights, it is also about our duties. Political participation is not only a right but also a duty. Contributing towards the common good of our society is not an individual choice but an obligation. That is why Cicero's work *On Duties* is his most important text, and in *On*

Duties we find some of the same themes we encounter in his text *On Old Age*. Perhaps this is not a coincidence considering that Cicero wrote both texts in the same year, 44 BC.

In *On Duties* Cicero suggests that all our duties are directed to one thing: the common good, which for Cicero is the same as the Roman Republic. What is important to emphasize here is that according to Cicero we are not exempt from these duties in old age. Thus, not only in an advanced age are we still capable of making a contribution to the common good, but we must make a contribution, and because of our experience, wisdom and higher intellect we are better placed to make a contribution in our old age compared to earlier stages in our lives.

But that's not all. Cicero makes two important observations about life in old age. First, he says: 'Old age has its appropriate weapons: namely the study, and the practice, of decent, enlightened living. Do all you can to develop these activities all your life, and as it draws to a close the harvest you reap will be amazing.'[17] Later he goes on to say: 'But please bear in mind ... old age must have its foundations well laid in early life.'[18]

These two deceivingly simple sentences pack a punch. What Cicero is telling us here is that everything we enjoy in old age is the fruit of our labour (mental and physical exercise) during our youth. In other words, our civic duties towards the common good applies to every stage of our lives, even in old age. This undermines the assumption on which the temporal view of reciprocity is based, namely that we contribute at time T1 to receive in T2. According to Cicero, we contribute both in T1 and T2, and in fact our contribution is greater in T2 than in T1. But in order to contribute at T2 there are sacrifices to be made at T1.

Importantly, Cicero also tells us that we all have a duty in the early part of our lives to do our best to be as healthy and strong and financially independent as we can be in our old age, and that this duty should not be eclipsed by claims of rights as we enter old age. In youth we want to exercise our right to drink and smoke and eat excessively, but let's not forget that we also have a duty to stay healthy throughout our entire life, and this requires moderation in our habits.

So here we get to the crux of Cicero's republican view on old age. The current emphasis on rights in moral and political theory has made us blind to our duties. The lesson we can take from Cicero's philosophical treatise *On Old Age* is that the overwhelming emphasis on the special rights we are entitled to in old age has meant that we no longer consider old age as a period in our lives when we still have duties, specifically the duty to make a meaningful contribution to the common good. We also forget that we have duties during our youth to ourselves in old age, and to the rest of our community who will look after us. Not acknowledging the ability of people living in old age to be able to contribute to society is disrespectful, and offensive, and potentially an injustice.

Conclusion

It would be a mistake to assume that in ancient times philosophers had a more benevolent view of old age. That was certainly not the case with Aristotle who, as Audrey Anton reminds us, not only associated old age with the physical maladies of decay, but also how it made people selfish, morally weak, and practically sociopathic:

Aristotle famously penned vitriolic remarks concerning the nature of the elderly ... Aristotle tells us that the older person is cowardly, distrusting, cheap, and inactive. The aged are loquacious, often subjecting others to protracted speeches and storytelling about the past. They are too fond of themselves. They do not love sincerely. They care almost exclusively for what is useful and very little (if at all) for what is noble.[19]

Cicero's views on old age are idiosyncratic, and the exact antithesis of Aristotle's. He encourages us to resist the discriminatory sirens of ageism and to reject the stigma associated with old age. Fundamentally, Cicero reminds us that life is to be lived till the very end, and that there is value to be extracted from life until the last moment. Writing in the sixteenth century, Michel de Montaigne summed it up perfectly when he said that Cicero gives one an appetite for growing old.

There is a growing literature today on the benefits of a gardening project for people with dementia. Publishing in the journal *Nursing Times*, Jeanette McClellan tells the story of staff at two nursing homes in Scotland in 2016 who set up a gardening project with the aim of improving outcomes for residents: 'One of the priorities was to get older people to be more active, as it is recognised that physical activity in that age group helps slow down physical and mental health deterioration.'[20] Many care homes today are following the same example, and the idea of creating a therapeutic gardening environment for people with dementia has become very popular.

Not many people realize that encouraging horticultural practices for people of an advanced age is precisely what Cicero was recommending in 44 BC. Towards the end of his treatise *On Old Age*,

Cicero has a lengthy analysis of the joys of farming, an activity that 'comes closest of all things to a life of true wisdom', and one that old age does not impede in the least: 'Well, this good fortune of practising agriculture and horticulture is one which an old man is able to enjoy: the cultivation of the soil is one of the activities which age does not impede up to his very last days.'[21] This is reassuring. Perhaps Cicero's most famous catchphrase is 'where there is life there is hope': this ode to optimism applies to everyone, in all stages of life, even in old age. In fact, especially in old age.

6

Rome needs philosophy

A mind without instruction can no more bear fruit than can a field,
however fertile, without cultivation.

MARCUS TULLIUS CICERO (TUSCULAN DISPUTATIONS)

Does the world need yet another book on Ancient Rome? Always. To anyone who doesn't understand why some people still go on about Ancient Rome, or ancient Romans, I recommend they watch the famous Monty Python sketch from *Life of Brian* (1979): 'What have the Romans ever done for us?' When John Cleese asks that question, the first answer to come back is 'the aqueduct!'. That is probably the right answer, since this astonishing feat of civil engineering remains one of the marvels of the ancient world.[1] The aqueduct is only the first of a long list of plausible answers to the question 'What have the Romans ever done for us?'.

Personally, if asked the same question, I would not hesitate to answer: 'the Roman Republic!'. This experiment in political governance is the bedrock of all our modern democracies. All the key concepts and institutions in modern politics that we value, treasure, and ill-advisedly take for granted can be traced back to the Roman Republic. As Melissa Lane points out, 'the ancient Greeks and Romans gave birth to a vocabulary still at work in the analyses and aspirations of many of those concerned with politics across the globe today'.[2] The Roman Republic is to politics what the aqueduct was to civil engineering: a daring project of spectacular optimism and ingenuity. Two-and-a-half thousand years ago, to theorize and practice governance in terms of a constitutional republican framework was as audacious as the staggering idea of carrying water on top of multiple arches for 40 miles from its source to an urban centre. And yet it was done.

But even if we accept that there is always room for another book on Ancient Rome, does the world really need another book on Cicero? Yes. Not only is Cicero today one of the great unsung heroes of antiquity, certainly in comparison to the persistent interest and adulation Julius Caesar still receives, but at a time when democracy is seriously under threat, Cicero is the perfect role model for the type of politician the world badly needs.

Unfortunately, Cicero is not a fashionable figure in contemporary political philosophy. Perhaps this is because for many centuries he was admired principally for his work on rhetoric, a skill no longer taught in school, or valued in society. When it wasn't rhetoric, historically Cicero was admired for advocating the law of nature, as if he were a precursor of Thomism and Christian philosophy.[3] When natural law theory lost its grip on moral philosophy, Cicero's political philosophy was gradually marginalized, and forgotten.

The emphasis on rhetoric and natural law theory is perhaps one reason why today Cicero still tends to be associated with the political ideology of conservatism. The fact that Cicero also received a positive endorsement from Edmund Burke, the eighteenth-century philosopher of conservatism par excellence, had the effect of boosting the reputation of Cicero as a conservative thinker. It is therefore not surprising to find that Neal Wood suggests that Cicero's political outlook typified a particular approach to civic affairs, namely the conservative mentality. According to Wood, for Cicero nothing should be done to alter the state or to upset the status quo, which explains why in Wood's view Cicero always opted for moderation and caution.[4]

I want to suggest a different reading of Cicero. Of course, Cicero was not and could never be deemed a radical, or a forerunner to Karl Marx or revolutionary politics. Not surprisingly, Marx and Engels didn't have much time for Cicero. Friedrich Engels viewed Cicero as 'the most contemptible scoundrel in history',[5] while Marx said that Cicero knew as little about philosophy as about the president of the United States of North America. The fact that Cicero was admired by John Locke, David Hume and Adam Smith does not make Cicero an obvious household name in socialist circles. And yet, I believe Cicero's work ought to be reread, and reassessed, to offer political guidance not of a conservative nature. In particular, notwithstanding some major lacunas and obvious limitations in his theorizing, Cicero remains an important author for anyone interested in promoting a more egalitarian, progressive society, and above all knowing how to protect and strengthen our democratic institutions.

The aim of this book is to change our perception of Cicero, and to offer a more progressive interpretation of Cicero's political thought, even if this means sacrificing historical accuracy. I'm less interested in figuring out what were Cicero's true intentions when he took a certain political decision or wrote a speech or philosophical treatise; there is already a plethora of excellent research published by many scholars in departments of classics to that effect. My goal is to apply the spirit of his ideas to our own historical context today, even if doing so requires taking some poetic licence with the historical figure of Cicero. In other words, the question is not to work out what was going on in Cicero's mind when he was writing a speech, a letter, a book, or taking a political decision. Instead, what we should ask ourselves is whether Cicero is still relevant in the twenty-first century. Does Cicero still speak to us today? I think he does, and I think we should listen to him.[6]

Cicero to the rescue

Modern democracies are in danger, and their chief enemy is an amalgam of authoritarianism and populism. This menace would have been very familiar to Cicero, which is why we still have a lot to learn from his political theory. A report published in November 2021 by the International Institute for Democracy and Electoral Assistance (IDEA) shows that a growing number of countries are sliding towards authoritarianism. Overall, the number of countries moving in an authoritarian direction in 2020 outnumbered those going in a democratic direction. This includes established democracies such as the United States, but also EU Member States including Hungary, Poland and Slovenia. At least four democracies have disappeared in the last two years, replaced by authoritarian regimes, either through flawed elections or military coups. The Global State of Democracy

(GSoD) indices show that authoritarian regimes have increased their repression, with 2020 being the worst year on record.[7]

To halt the slide towards authoritarianism there are several measures that need to be either reinforced or implemented. These include: a proper separation of power so that there are clear checks and balances between the different branches of government; an impartial administration that is corruption-resistant, or at the very least where corruption is not tolerated; a high level of participatory engagement in all levels of civil society and government; an ethical approach to politics where the common good trumps selfish individualism; a serious effort to tackle occurrences of domination across all sectors of society; a system that exposes populist demagoguery for what it is and eradicates fake news; a diminution in the levels of social and economic inequality across society. All of the above are issues where Cicero had a great deal to say.

In a letter to Marcus Brutus written in June 43 BC, a mere six months before Cicero's assassination, Cicero gives an accurate account of the end of the Roman Republic: 'Everybody demands as much political power as he has force behind him. Reason, moderation, law, tradition, duty count for nothing – likewise the judgement and views of the citizen body and respect for the opinion of those who come after us.'[8] As we enter the third decade of the twenty-first century, this sounds worryingly familiar. If we want to avoid making the same mistakes as our Roman ancestors did around 44 BC, if we want to keep hold of our democratic institutions, if we want to stop authoritarianism from taking over, we could do a lot worse than to read, reread and learn from Cicero.

There are many important principles and ideas we can uncover, or rediscover, from reading Cicero's books, speeches and letters, but there is also another aspect of Cicero's life that I think ought to be emphasized, and appreciated, the driving force behind all his endeavours: his love of philosophy, his conviction that philosophy matters and his faith that philosophy can influence the course of history.

In Chapter 2, we saw how in *On Duties* Cicero considered the crisis of the Roman Republic as a moral crisis as well as a political crisis. The main actors who precipitated the collapse of the Republic, including Julius Caesar and Marc Antony, were culpable of being morally weak and inadequate. This is where philosophy becomes invaluable, performing a major role in fortifying the Republic. Katharina Volk perfectly captures the spirit of Cicero's political activism:

> What Rome needs, badly, are men who, like Brutus and Cassius, know how to act virtuously and those who, like Cicero, can explain to their fellow citizens what virtuous behavior is. In other words, Rome needs philosophy.[9]

The truth is that today we need philosophy as much as Rome needed philosophy back then.

Learning democracy

There is an interesting parallel to be drawn between the parabolic trajectory of the Roman Republic and that of modern democracies. Both started life as utopian aspirations, before evolving into legitimate claims, then heroic ideals worth dying for and finally, tragically, to a culture of egotism and greediness, gelled together by the imperative to be amused. Today, in our age of instant gratification where screens reign supreme, the biggest challenge is how to convey the message that democracy is no laughing matter, and it demands our serious attention.

In a democracy voters have the right to vote, and that's how it should be, but now they also expect to be entertained for taking the trouble of performing their civic duties. If the eighteenth century was the Age of Reason, today we live in the Age of Entertainment. In the global theatre of democratic politics, buffoonery has been elevated first to an art form, and then to a political-catalyst. In the UK, former Prime Minister Boris Johnson was cunning enough to understand that to succeed in politics today it is more important to be amusing and whacky rather than competent or honest. In America, on pure entertainment value, there was only going to be one winner in the 2016 Presidential election between Donald Trump and Hillary Clinton.

Democracy is not just an institutional system; it is also a culture. To strengthen democracy one needs not only the right laws, one also needs the right form of political education. Unfortunately, culture takes time and effort. Developing a democratic culture is a slow process, requiring a lot of patience and a good dose of toleration. Deliberation is what democracies are essentially about, and the process of deliberation involves taking time to listen to others, to evaluate their arguments, to ponder before civilly responding – all the skills that define sound philosophical engagement. The philosophical method is indistinguishable from the democratic method. But few people have time for democracy anymore, and even less for philosophy. Today we have lost the required virtue of civility and patience that is the beating heart of the democratic ethos.

Cicero truly believed that the best remedy against authoritarianism was to educate the youth, and that philosophy should be central to their education. For Cicero there was no greater or better service to the state than to educate Romans through philosophy, which is why Cicero embarked on the project of writing about Greek philosophy in Latin, and in the process adapting Greek philosophy to the Roman context, as well as inventing the necessary Latin terminology to convey certain Greek terms and ideas. Cicero saw philosophy as a discipline with the power to change lives. As Raphael Woolf says, 'His aim is to make his fellow citizens more educated, and he sees this as a form of service comparable to his engagement in public affairs'.[10]

At the same time Cicero also believed in the symbiotic relationship between a good state and good philosophy, an idea perfectly captured by Neal Wood:

> The state provides an environment conducive to the flourishing of culture and its highest manifestation, philosophy. Without the state, philosophy would not have been born, and without philosophy's guidance the state is like a rudderless ship.[11]

On this note, it is worth remembering Cicero's uncompromising critique of Epicurus, the Greek philosopher, in part because Cicero may have had more than Epicurus on his mind when he wrote those lines: 'a man without science, without letters, one who insults all, without critical ability, without weight, without wit'.[12] If one didn't know that Cicero was writing about Epicurus, and had to guess who was at the receiving end of Cicero's tirade, a number of people come to mind. Certainly Catiline, Clodius or Marc Antony, possibly Pompey: all would-be dictators, all lacking culture. He fought them in the Forum, and when he was prevented from doing so, he fought them in his books. This is why Cicero not only delivered some of the most memorable speeches in the history of Ancient Rome, but he also wrote them down, and distributed them, for the benefit of his friends, fellow citizens and (why not) posterity.

Zvi Yavetz is right when he suggests that Cicero was not a philosopher or even an intellectual in politics, instead Cicero can best be described as an intellectual politician, a man of letters: 'Nobody can deny that he was a man of letters par excellence, and as such he faced the same problems as philosophers in antiquity or intellectuals in politics in our own days.'[13] We don't necessarily need more philosophers in politics (although it wouldn't do any harm), but we certainly need more women and men of letters in politics.

Philosophy, for Cicero, can be subversive and constructive in equal measures. As a substitute for direct political participation, philosophy is a powerful form of political activism. Raphael Woolf reminds us that Cicero speaks of the writing of philosophy on a par with more traditional forms of service to the state:

> When he thought he had substituted philosophy for government, it was 'in my books' that he delivered his senatorial opinions and his speeches to assemblies. Writing philosophy becomes a way ... of discharging the functions of practical politics themselves.[14]

Philosophy for Cicero is always constructive, to the extent that it plays a key role in educating us about values of the Republic. The issue here is not the creation of that ephemeral creature 'the philosopher-king', but instead, and more importantly, the engendering of the committed citizen. In fact, in true republican spirit, for Cicero creating the right sort of citizen is more important than fabricating the right leader. That's why we need books, and culture, and why we also need more philosophy. Ultimately, I think Cicero would have approved of Umberto Eco's claim, from his novel *The Name of the Rose*, that 'we live for books. A sweet mission in this world dominated by disorder and decay'.[15]

Cicero believed that philosophy should be central to everyone's education, including politicians, and that it is through the study of philosophy that citizens come to understand their civic and democratic duties, grounded on the ideal of a common good. As Cicero says in *De Inventione Rhetorica* (On Rhetorical Invention), written in 84 BC when he was still a young man, anyone who neglects the study of philosophy and moral conduct will develop 'into something useless to himself and harmful to his country'.[16] Philosophy, like democracy, thrives where there is disagreement and deliberation, where there is no appeal to authority, where fallibilism is embraced, and where disputes are not resolved by force or diktat. In his *Tusculan Disputations*, Book 2, Cicero reminds us that the strength of philosophy is acquired from the disagreements and conflicts characteristic of philosophical debates, and all those who believe to have certainty on their side are the enemies of philosophy, and democracy.

Cicero's failings

In this book, I have done my best to restore the reputation of Cicero as a significant figure, and not just historically. I have argued that Cicero, the philosopher-cum-politician, represents a type of statesman that is long gone but still badly needed. In that sense, Cicero can still be a role model for us today.

Of course, this doesn't mean that Cicero was faultless, or that his political vision was beyond criticism. There is no doubt that his political philosophy had considerable blind spots. In Chapter 3, I argued that equality was as important to Cicero as liberty, in fact that liberty is meaningless unless it's equal liberty. However, his conception of equality was undertheorized. While he appreciated the importance of moral equality and equality before the law, he seems to have no appreciation of the importance of substantive or economic equality. Neal Wood makes the point that there is contradiction in Cicero's political thought, with Cicero's deep and lasting belief in the moral equality of human beings at odds with his acceptance in theory and practice of an inegalitarian society: 'A sincere and dedicated egalitarian in moral principles, he is unquestionably an inegalitarian in social and political theory.'[17]

Cicero was blind, as many senators in Rome were at the time, to the abject living conditions of the masses. He did not fully understand the desperation of the plebeians. The fact that he uses the term *faeces* to refer to the lower classes speaks for itself; this term is usually translated as 'dregs of society' although it literally means 'sewage' or 'shit'.[18] Cicero's Rome was not a place where politics was always resolved by rational discourse, as philosophers would wish. Instead, it was a brutal society where violence was the currency of everyday politics. This reality is the premise of Richard Alston's important book on the end of the Roman Republic:

> The great truth of history, so often unspoken, is that for most of our ancestors the key issues were not those of political philosophy, the nature of freedom and the nation, but how to feed oneself and one's children. *History is about food.*[19]

What Cicero's political philosophy lacks is a theory of distributive justice, in fact writing a book on Cicero's theory of economic justice could possibly turn into the world's shortest book. Furthermore, he seemed to be almost uninterested in economic analysis, or even political economy. It is therefore not a surprise that the populist politics of Julius Caesar, centred around free bread and spectacular festival and games, were a hit with the Roman masses. As the poet Juvenal (first-century AD) writes in his *Satire*, 10.77–81, the common people no longer care about their freedom, no longer have a sense of civic duty, but are only interested in bread and circuses, *panem et circenses*.

Because he was not a military man, Cicero failed to understand that the most powerful class in Rome at the end of the Republic were the Roman soldiers, the often-neglected underclass of Roman society, who signed up to war to avoid starvation but were not afraid to use violence or switch allegiance between warring factions if the material remunerations they had been promised did not materialize.[20]

Cicero's lack of class consciousness is not surprising, given that politics at the time was not ideological but strictly personal. Politics was not run by political parties, distinguished by ideological positions, but by strong personalities. Voters gave their allegiance and trust to candidates based on their personal interactions with them, not on the basis of a political programme or manifesto. Nevertheless, Cicero always assumed that the masses would be dumbfounded by the brilliance of his oratory, forgetting that they also needed adequate food and shelter. Ideals are important, but they are useless when it comes to feeding your children. Cicero's lack of economic realism was a major lacuna in his politics.

Cicero has also been castigated for his arrogance. In one of the least distinguished books on Roman history ever written, Boris Johnson (yes, *that* Boris Johnson) has this to say about Cicero: 'The trouble with Cicero is that, for all his rhetorical brilliance, he was a second-rate politician. ... He bored for Rome about the importance of the old way of doing things; he loathed the militarism and opportunism of Caesar. He was fundamentally right, *but always let down by his own vanity and self-importance*.'[21] The hypocrisy of this statement is astounding. For Boris Johnson to accuse anyone of vanity and self-importance beggars belief.

Such criticism of Cicero is too simplistic, and profoundly misguided, although still very common. For a man not blessed with being born into a patrician family in Rome, hampered by a physical and moral disposition that made a military career beyond his reach, Cicero's only comparative advantage vis-à-vis his more fortunate peers were his intellect and hard work. And yes, perhaps at times he let his tongue, and wit, get the better of him, but it wasn't a simple case of narcissism. I believe Richard Alston gets it right when he says that Cicero 'had a typically Roman fondness for display and acclaim, and from time to time he appears to have been dazzled by his own brilliance'.[22] There is no doubt that at times Cicero's facility with words got him into trouble, as we are about to see, but that didn't make him a second-rate politician.

Death by witticism

One of the things that stands out in Cicero's speeches, especially those he delivered in a legal context, were his jokes. Humour is one of the highest forms of culture, and arguably its sharpest weapon. Cicero prevailed over many dangerous and powerful figures in Rome by making fun of them. His personal letters are also very amusing, but his humour, often self-deprecating, always carried a sting; as Amanda Wilcox rightly points out, 'even the most exuberant joking passages include topical political content'.[23] When Julius Caesar all but suspended free speech, after becoming dictator, Cicero used satire in his private correspondence to retain some semblance of licence to speak.

Living at a time when honour and reputation were inexorably connected with success in the battlefield, Cicero's lack of military training was a major handicap to his political ambitions. A declared pacifist, Cicero's squeamishness at the sight of blood would have been held against him. Cicero was possibly the only Roman of his time who detested gladiatorial fights, something that would have been seen as a clear mark of deficiency in his basic leadership credentials. And yet, notwithstanding his humble origins, and against all odds, he succeeded.

Only ten 'new men' (a person who lacked senatorial ancestors) reached the consulship in the last 150 years of the Roman Republic, and Cicero was the only one to achieve this between 93 and 48 BC.[24] Behind Cicero's success we find his immense intellect (and initially his wife's dowry). He used his brilliant mind, and unsurpassed mastery of the Latin language, to score points against his enemies. The metonymic adage 'the pen is mightier than the sword' perfectly captures Cicero: his written and spoken words allowed him to rise above the violence of the dagger. Cicero considered jokes as 'weapons of war'.[25]

When confronted with an adversary in the Senate or the Forum, Cicero proved to be an unsurpassed master in the art of character assassination. He would cut his enemies down to size joke by joke. The speeches he gave against Marc Antony in 44 and 43 BC, towards the end of his life, are legendary. These speeches are known as the 'Philippics', and they are as powerful and entertaining today as they were when they were first spoken. Throughout his life Cicero used humour to disarm his adversaries. Early on in his long career, during a debate in the Senate on the distribution of land in Campania to Caesar's soldiers, a very old senator called Lucius Gellius stood up and proclaimed: 'this law will not pass for as long as I live!', to which Cicero replied, 'Let us wait, then, since Gellius does not ask us to postpone things for long.'[26]

Unfortunately, he wasn't always able to tell the difference between a good joke and a bad joke. Undoubtedly, Cicero's most unwise, shameful decision in his entire life was to remarry in 45 BC: he was sixty, and his new wife Publilia was only fourteen or fifteen. Rome was a very permissive society, and yet this nuptial surprised many people, and even shocked a few. When the age difference was brought to his attention the night before his wedding, Cicero retorted: 'She'll be a grown-up woman tomorrow.'[27] This isn't even funny, and while his actions may not have been illegal, they are certainly morally unacceptable. There is no justification for Cicero's conduct on this matter. Thankfully, he realized the errors of his judgement and divorced her after only a few months.

There are good reasons to believe that he married Publilia not for her youth, or to satisfy his carnal desires, but because she was rich. To be politically active in Rome one needed money, and marriage was a standard way to attain financial security. Of course this does not excuse Cicero, nor make his behaviour less deplorable; as Susan

Treggiari rightly says: 'He had treated his young wife cruelly: no excuse is possible.'[28] We know very little about women in Ancient Rome, since to the best of our knowledge they did not write books or kept diaries, or if they did none survived. This is why Treggiari's book on the three women in Cicero's life (his first wife Terentia, his daughter Tullia, and his second wife Publilia) is a must read for anyone interested in Cicero, or more generally in women in Ancient Rome.

Cicero's insensitive remark towards his new wife on his wedding day is a reminder that he simply could not resist a pun, and not always in good taste.[29] His trusted secretary and friend Tito collected Cicero's many jokes over a lifetime in three volumes.[30] It was said that Cicero preferred to lose friends rather than a joke; as it turned out, Cicero lost a lot more than friends because of his wit. In the end, it was a bad joke that cost him his life.

Following the death of Julius Caesar, the young Octavian was challenging Marc Antony for supreme leadership of the Republic. He was barely nineteen years old. Referring to Octavian, who within a few years became known as emperor Augustus, Cicero said: 'the young man was to be praised, rewarded – and elevated', in Latin: *laudandum adolescentem, ornandum, tollendum*. The last word *tollendum* has a double meaning, which is probably the reason Cicero chose this term, just for the sake of making a pun. According to Anthony Trollope, *tollendum* could be translated as 'elevated to the skies, or to the gallows'.[31] Kathryn Tempest suggests a slightly different translation: Octavian ought to be praised, applauded and pushed. Here 'pushed' has a double meaning: 'Octavian could be pushed further in his ambitions (i.e. elevated), or he could be pushed aside (i.e. discarded).[32] The implication being that Octavian should be supported for the sake of defeating Marc Antony, but then Octavian should be cast aside and the Roman Republic restored. In the novel *Dictator*, the third volume of his fictionalized biography of Cicero's life, Robert Harris uses the more poetic translation 'raised, praised, erased': the ambiguity of *tollendum* is lost, but the rhyme is seductive.

Cicero's witticism reached Octavian, who was not impressed. A few months later Octavian and Marc Antony reached a truce, and they agreed on a list of 'enemies of the state' to be executed – the proscriptions of 43 BC. Cicero's name was one of the first to be added to the fatal list, his death sentence signed. Within a short space of time Cicero was dead, his head decapitated. Cicero had a deadly sense of humour, but on this occasion it tragically backfired.

Conclusion

To that tiny minority of people familiar with Cicero's life and work, his influence on Western culture is well known and duly acknowledged. The impact of Cicero's work on Humanism, the major intellectual movement of the Renaissance, is beyond dispute.[33] Humanism, which stressed the importance of reason and dignity in our common humanity, became the dominant intellectual movement in Europe in the sixteenth century. Without Cicero, Humanism may not have happened. Many influential writers and thinkers we associate with

Humanism, including Michel de Montaigne, Hugo Grotius and Samuel von Pufendorf, were greatly indebted to Cicero's writings.[34]

The Enlightenment took over where Humanism left off, and once again we find that many of the most important Enlightenment thinkers, including John Locke, Jean-Jacques Rousseau, Montesquieu, David Hume, Adam Smith, Immanuel Kant and John Adams were influenced by Cicero. While a minority of Enlightenment thinkers tackled Cicero's writing directly, the vast majority of them merely took inspiration from Cicero. As Matthew Fox explains, in part that's because, unlike most other Enlightenment philosophers, 'Cicero is not himself a systematic thinker, nor one whose works lend themselves easily to the production of a clear social or political programme'.[35] Cicero's influence over the centuries is beyond doubt, even though today we seem to have forgotten about this 'new man' from Arpinium who had the courage to stand up to a long list of populist-inclined dictators, someone who did everything in his powers to halt the advent of authoritarianism. He was murdered for his efforts.

The fact that Cicero achieved what he did, notwithstanding starting life with the handicap of being a 'new man', is relevant to us today. He always felt he was being treated as the 'Other', as if 'new men' and the patricians were entirely different breeds of men.[36] This prejudice, bordering on racism, will be familiar today to any member of a minority group. At least Cicero had the advantage of being born a man, since in Ancient Rome women were excluded from both politics and civil society. What Cicero experienced can be compared to the epistemic injustice many women endure in the workplace today; to the unconscious bias experienced by immigrants and refugees, or anyone with a foreign accent and a foreign name; to the discrimination, intentional or unintentional, against members of the LGBT+ community. Today the barriers to social mobility are much higher than we like to admit, and meritocracy remains a ludicrous myth.

Epilogue: Why read Cicero today

> *O tempora, o mores!*
> *Oh what times! Oh what customs!*
> MARCUS TULLIUS CICERO (*AGAINST CATILINE*)

In the twenty-first century, the refugee and migrant crisis has become perhaps the most divisive, and disturbing, global political reality.[1] Every state and every continent is turning into a fortress, doing their worst to deny citizenship to refugees. It may surprise some readers to find that Cicero was in favour of extending citizenship, not restricting it, since he recognized that this was in the interest of the Roman Republic: 'We should increase this state by welcoming even those who had been our enemies. ... Our ancestors never let the opportunity of granting and sharing their citizenship pass.'[2] It is truly remarkable, and a credit to Cicero, that 2,000 years ago he had the foresight to think of ethics in cosmopolitan terms.[3]

There are three political questions where Cicero can still speak to us: the advance of far-right populism; the corrosive nature of corruption; and our abdication of duties as citizens.

The resurgence of the populist far-right

The far-right is on the rise, everywhere. Populism today is founded on a specific but crude and somewhat distorted understanding of the social and political landscape where only two political groupings exist: the perfidious elite, holders of the reins of political and economic power, and the excluded masses. This appraisal of social dynamics, constructed around a simple dichotomy, has a long history. The Romans organized their affairs around two mutually exclusive social ranks, patricians and plebeians. There is nothing new about this political phenomenon: already rife in Ancient Rome, populism is as old as politics itself. Contrary to what is generally believed, populism is not a bottom-up political movement, the desperate voice of the marginalized masses, the political expression of a final, radical, democratic push by those who for too long have been excluded, and they are not going to take it any more. Instead, populism is a top-down phenomenon, nothing more than covert elitism.

Populism arises in the context of a clash between ruling elites: it is the articulation of a calculated political strategy used by one section of the elite in order to gain the upper hand on a different section of the elite. In the last analysis, populism can be explained in terms of the masses being instigated and manipulated by some members of the elite in pursuit of their own interests. Seen in this light, populism is a tried and tested political strategy. Liberal democracies are not immune from demagogues and populists. Just like in Ancient Rome, modern leaders of right-wing populist movements almost always emerge from privileged backgrounds.

As we saw in Chapter 3, Cicero distinguished *populus* (the people) from *popularis*, the latter being much closer to the term 'populism' in today's lexicon. Cicero had a complex relationship with the concept of *popularis*, a term that is politically charged and ambiguous, especially in the hands of Cicero who redefined the term during his long career to suit his interests. It has been calculated that Cicero used the word *popularis* (or related words) 244 times in his extant works: 42 per cent in positive terms (often applying the word to himself), less than a quarter of his uses are negative, and the remaining third either neutral or ambiguous.[4]

Cicero approved of *popularis* when he needed to remind the political elite in Rome that the Republic must be for the common good of the people, *all* the people, and the Senate must not make the mistake of presuming to be above the rest of the citizens. But *popularis* was a term Cicero also used disapprovingly to highlight the risk to the Republic of populist politicians. It is interesting to note that Cicero had sympathy, in principle, for the agrarian reforms of Tiberius and Gaius Gracchus, and had high praise for the oratory of Gaius Gracchus. At the same time, he disapproved of their political methods, which he found deeply divisive.

In *On the Republic* Cicero observed that the tribunate of Tiberius Gracchus in 133 BC 'split a single people into two camps'.[5] In Latin, it reads: *divisit populum unum in duas partis* (Rep. I.31). The idea that the people (*populum*), which as we know is the state (*res publica res populi*), is divided in two parts, was highly problematic for Cicero. He also accuses Gaius Gracchus of inciting violence against the state, once again dividing the people: 'Take Gaius Gracchus. Through his tribunate, and through those daggers which he claimed to have tossed into the forum to make the citizens fight like gladiators with one another, did he not overturn the entire state of the country?'[6]

Two thousand years ago, Cicero had already understood that populist politics only brought out the worst in people, as his letter to his friend Atticus referring to the first triumvirate of Julius Caesar, Pompey and Crassus testifies: 'those "populist" politicians have taught even quiet folk to hiss'.[7] We must not forget this lesson, nor lower our guard against modern populists. The divisive nature of populist politics, including the incitement to violence, is something we are familiar with in the twenty-first century. The assault on the United States Capitol on 6 January 2021 will go down in history as one of the darkest chapters in American politics.

Cicero devoted his life to resisting, criticizing and trying to prevent military coups orchestrated by populist politicians. Catiline, Clodius, Julius Caesar: all populists, all involved in military plots to overthrow the Roman Republic and establish themselves as sole dictators. Perhaps his greatest foe was Publius Clodius Pulcher, the man who forced Cicero into exile in 58 BC. Cicero refers to Clodius's tribunate as 'the reign of terror'. Cicero quickly understood that populism was nothing more than a political strategy, which some politicians from privileged backgrounds use to advance their own political ends. This strategy was implemented by instigating divisiveness, via the use of violence, to demolish the existing order.

Cicero always believed that unity not divisiveness was in the best interest of the people of Rome. Unity is a recurring theme in Cicero's work. At the start of his career, he argued for the need for co-operation and concord between the highest-ranking citizens of the state, namely the senators and the equestrians, but this political ideal could be expanded to include all classes in society, all citizens, all people. Cicero coined the term *concordia ordinum*, the harmony of the orders, to capture this political ideal of unity. This project was initially meant for two groups, or classes, in society: the senators, who represented the nobility in Roman society but were not allowed to engage in business or trade, and the equestrians, the very rich high middle-class businessmen and traders. Cicero believed that the survival of the Republic rested on this unity, and he saw populists as a threat to unity, and therefore as a threat to the Republic.

According to Cicero, the only people who stood to gain from the fractious politics of populism and the radical changes it championed were the leaders of these movements, not the people. He made his views clear in an important speech at the start of his consulship against the agrarian reform favoured by two leading populist politicians, Crassus and Julius Caesar: 'They pretend they are acting in the people's interests when they make their speeches, but really they are acting against the interests, and even the safety, of the people.'[8]

It was a wave of authoritarian populism that ultimately brought the Roman Republic to its knees, and a similar fate may befall our democracies. These are dangerous times we live in, not dissimilar to what Cicero experienced in his time. Although Cicero was unable to save the Roman Republic from populism and authoritarianism, there are still many things we can learn from him today to avoid making the same mistake as our Roman ancestors.

Cicero believed that strong, just institutions were the best antidote against right-wing populism, executed via the rule of law, constitutional procedures, and the reinforcement of a system of checks and balances. But to counter the appeal of populism he also recommended two strategies necessary for promoting justice and reinforcing mutual trust. First, by creating a sense of solidarity and community amongst citizens. In his philosophical essay *On Friendship*, the topic of Chapter 4, Cicero writes that true friendship is never instrumental, nor is it grounded on weakness. He echoes the same insight in his political treatise *On the Republic*, analysed in Chapter 3, where he states that the primary reason for the public coming together to form a republic is not weakness but a desire on the part of human beings to form communities. The problem is that we have lost our sense of community; too many people today no longer see each other as friends pursuing a common goal, instead they prioritize narrow-minded interests spurred by a divisive, parochial sense of identity.

Secondly, Cicero argues that justice and trust cannot flourish where inequalities abound. Liberty is the central notion of a republic, but as Cicero reminds us, if it isn't equal throughout, it isn't liberty at all. He goes on to explain that a mixed constitution has, in the first place, a widespread element of equality. One of the problems with our society today is not only the growing inequalities within each nation state but also the inequality across nation states. Global neoliberal policies of austerity have exasperated the problem.

Modern democracies are not immune from the populist threat. To some extent we are the architects of our own downfall. We need to go back to basics, which is where Cicero comes in. There is a simple message that we can take from Cicero's philosophical works and political experience: corruption is a form of political cancer which weakens the fabric of democracy. Corruption is also the oxygen on which populism thrives.

Corruption

Where there is politics there is corruption. There is corruption in autocracies, and there is corruption in democracies. But the inevitability of corruption does not mean that we must accept it. How a political system responds to corruption is a valid litmus test for its democratic credentials.

Ancient Rome was rife with corruption. Bribery could often secure a favourable outcome in the court of law, notwithstanding the crushing evidence against the accused, as in the case of Clodius in 61 BC. In the aftermath of the *Bona Dea* scandal, when Clodius infiltrated the women-only religious festival dressed as a woman, the trial pitted Clodius against Cicero. The evidence was overwhelming and yet Clodius walked free: a scandalous amount of bribery paid by Crassus, Rome's riches man and a close political ally of Julius Caesar, ensured Clodius's release. Cicero's views on the jury in that trial speak for themselves: 'There has never been a more disgraceful bunch of men in a low-grade music hall!'[9]

Being a republic rather than a monarchy meant that elections were a crucial mechanism of its political infrastructure, and elections were fertile ground for candidates with deep pockets. Electoral campaigns were very expensive, especially during the last few decades of the Republic, and candidates were forced to take massive loans which led to heavy debts. Bribery was the most efficient method of swaying voters.[10] Once elected, a politician would be rewarded with a stint as a governor in one of Rome's colonial outposts, or as leader of a military campaign. In either case the opportunities for corruption, extortion and enrichment were considerable. This was legalized looting on a grand scale, but since it occurred many miles away from Rome, it did not seem to matter.

Cicero belongs to that very small cohort of politicians in Rome at the time who won all his elections (four in total: *questor, aedile, praetor* and *consul*) without recourse to the use of bribery. He even took a public stand against corruption, and during his consulship passed a law increasing the penalty for electoral bribery to ten years' exile. As it transpired, this law turned out to be toothless, since those who were tried for corruption were constantly and inevitably found to be innocent after bribing the jury, but at least Cicero's intentions were honourable.

At the start of his career Cicero made anti-corruption his distinctive mission, an audacious gamble that was extremely risky and could have easily ended his political career even before it took off. Cicero came to prominence in Rome as a young lawyer, first as the defence council and then as prosecutor on two spectacular cases of corruption, which Cicero unexpectedly won. The first case, in 80 BC, was to defend Sextus Roscius who was unjustly charged with patricide. The accusation was fabricated with the complicity of a man called Chrysogonus, one of the most powerful, violent and corrupt men in Rome at the time, also dictator Sulla's ex-slave and right-hand man. The second case, in 70 BC, was the prosecution of Gaius Verres, who had been appointed the governor of Sicily in 73 BC, and whose conduct was so ruthless that his behaviour even shocked the people of Rome, who were generally extremely tolerant of all forms of extortions and other malpractices against non-Romans.

Cicero practiced what he preached. In 75 BC, he was elected as magistrate (*questor*) of the Roman Republic, and was allocated a post in Western Sicily, Rome's oldest province and strategically important for its supply of grain to Rome. People in his position were expected to abuse their considerable power to make a lucrative profit for themselves, instead Cicero surprised everyone by being honest, lenient and fair with his dealings with the locals, something that was unheard of in the corridors of power at the time. Cicero was possibly the first and last honest Roman politician to have graced one of the Roman provinces in official capacity. In 51 BC, Cicero did a second stint as the commander of a province, this time in Cilicia in Asia Minor (modern Turkey). Once again, he distinguished himself for his integrity, decency and sense of duty.

Corruption in Ancient Rome is legendary, but is politics today fundamentally different? There is as much corruption today as in the past, but it has become more discreet, inconspicuous, less unabashed, and thus our society has learned the art of concealing it. Marcus Licinius Crassus was a close political ally of Julius Caesar and one of the wealthiest men in the history of Rome. In the battle of Carrhae (today Harran, Turkey, in the Şanlıurfa Province) in 53 BC, he was defeated by general Surenas and his Parthian King Orodes II, and allegedly executed by having molten gold poured down his throat as punishment for his unquenchable thirst for wealth.

Peter Stothard gives a chilling account of this episode: 'The man tasked with delivering Crassus's head to Orodes was the local governor, Silaces ... [Crassus's] open mouth, shriveled by desert storm, had been filled with molten gold as testament to his lifetime greed, and that when Silaces brought the king his gift, the barbarian court was watching a performance of Euripides' last tragedy, *The Bacchae*, and that Crassus's head became a stage prop for the end of the show.'[11]

Politicians today are unlikely to experience the same fate as Crassus, although some of them are not less greedy, or corrupt.[12]

Our duties as citizens

Democracy and elections are synonymous in our collective imagination. Where there are no elections there is no democracy, and the unpredictable nature of elections is the reason why, procedurally speaking, democracy can neatly be defined in terms of 'institutionalized uncertainty'.[13]

When we compared liberal and republican conceptions of democracy in Chapter 3, we said that citizenship is defined principally in terms of rights, starting from the right to vote. Individual voters, and their rights, are the bastion of liberal democracy. But the liberal imprint on democracy is unduly permissive, its expectations on citizens living in a democracy far too meek, and as a result liberal democracy has gradually become oblivious to a simple truth: voting is much more than a right, or a privilege, it is also a duty. And as such it should be treated.

To be in a privileged position is to have an advantage or opportunity that most other people do not have. To be privileged is to be recognized as someone in authority, with decision-making powers. To think of voting as a right is to emphasize the freedom we enjoy to act upon our privileged position, or not, as one may choose. And voting is certainly a right. But there is also another way to think of a privilege, and that is in terms of a duty, or responsibility.

In *On Duties*, discussed in Chapter 2, Cicero tells us that we have two overarching duties: first, to seek out the truth and be truthful, and secondly, to preserve and uphold the structure of justice. Although Cicero did not write about voting as a duty, the spirit of his moral and political philosophy can be adapted to our concerns today: all voters privileged to live in a democracy have the duty to exercise their right to vote and to engage in the political process by making informed political decisions.

When Cicero says that we have a duty to 'the maintenance of social order and communal life among men',[14] and that we do this by 'securing relations of trust',[15] he is telling us that we have a duty to preserve and uphold the structure of justice and democracy. Cicero was not just referring to professional politicians, he was also thinking of the ordinary citizens. In modern democracies citizens have the opportunity and privilege to engage everyday with the life of the polity, and voting is one way of performing this duty.

It is a law of politics, if not nature, that in any political system voters have the knack to always blame the political class for everything that goes wrong, and never themselves. This is the essence of the blame fallacy: because something did not turn out as I intended, there must be someone else I can blame. Sometimes this is true of course, especially when people are very vulnerable and with very few options open to them, but that's not the case for the majority of people living in liberal democracies in rich, developed countries. Citizens and voters need to take some responsibility for the outcome of the democratic process, and consider their duties, blessed as they are with the rights and privileges to choose their political leaders.

The blame fallacy is a bottomless pit, and it is far too convenient to draw water from it. Accusations that all political parties and all politicians are the same are just lazy, irresponsible rhetoric. In the last analysis, in a democracy the legitimacy of ruling parties and governments comes from the voters and citizens, *res publica res populi.* The emphasis on the duties of citizenship is, of course, at the heart of Cicero's conception of republicanism and if Cicero were alive today, he would urge all citizens to take their duties seriously, by becoming more politically engaged, and to participate to the best of their ability in the life of the polis. And above all, to become more informed.

It takes time and effort to become politically literate, but it is our duty as citizens to do so. The duty to seek and uphold the truth certainly applies to our politicians, but it applies also to every voter and citizen in a democracy. The nature of lies, and the proclamations of liars, is a pressing problem, not least because lies are part of the DNA of modern society, except that we now refer to them with the more dignified terminology of 'marketing', 'advertising', 'propaganda' or 'spin'. From unscrupulous sellers of second-hand cars to prime ministers and presidents, it seems that these days everybody makes a living from lies.

This is nothing new of course. When in 64 BC Cicero ran for election to become a consul in the Roman Republic, his brother Quintus Tullius wrote a 'Little Handbook on Electioneering', *Commentariolum Petitionis,* where he recommends the use of truth, half-truths and direct lies, if and when necessary.[16] Nothing much has changed since then: fast forward 2,000 years, and in an essay published in *The New Yorker* in 1967, 'Truth and Politics', Hannah Arendt was still lamenting the fact that politics and truth don't mix: 'No one has ever doubted that truth and politics are on rather bad terms with each other, and no one, as far as I know, has ever counted truthfulness among the political virtues.'[17]

In the twenty-first century, the contempt some politicians have for truth appears to have reached new levels. But voters must also take a share in the blame: if the voters know that a certain politician is a liar, why do they choose to believe the politician? Why do voters vote for politicians that they know are liars? There seems to be a paradox here: the more the electorate claims to be exasperated by the crooked, fraudulent shenanigans of the political elite, the more they vote for them; the more politicians lie to voters, the more voters trust them. But in a democracy we have the power, and the duty, to change this trajectory, simply by casting our vote for truth. As Cicero said, we have a duty to truth.[18]

Conclusion

The global rise of the far-right today is not dissimilar from what Cicero experienced in Rome. Today, like 2,000 years ago in Rome, right-wing populist movements are jeopardizing the democratic foundations of the republic, posing a threat to the political system of check and balances, and opening the door to the politics of fear and intolerance.

Cicero was not able to rescue the Roman Republic from such threats, but with the help of philosophy he tried to oppose his enemies by putting trust in the authority of the rule of law. In *On Laws*, Book I, Cicero writes: 'Of all the issues dealt with in philosophical debates surely nothing is more vital than the clear realization that we are born for justice, and that what is just is based, not on opinion, but on nature.'[19] His lessons are still valid many centuries later, and precious to us as we face a similar set of challenges.

I started this book telling the story of a fictional girl disappointed not to find books on Cicero in her local bookshop. I wrote this book with that girl on my mind, clutching to the desperate hope that one day she, and her friends, will find more books on Cicero in bookshops. I want to live in a world where bookshops are full of books on Cicero, not Julius Caesar; where the remarkable scholarship on Cicero by authors like Gesine Manuwald, Malcolm Schofield, Kathryn Tempest, Katharina Volk and Raphael Woolf is easily available. I want to live in a world where in primary and secondary schools around the world, on posters hanging on classroom walls depicting Ancient Rome, next to the obligatory cut-out photos of the Colosseum we also find pictures of Cicero, the philosopher of the Roman Republic, and not Julius Caesar, the military general symbolizing dictatorships and empires.

This book was written in the spirit of Cicero's obstinate belief in democratic politics, and his unyielding sense of hope for a better future. If we don't want our modern democracies to end like the Roman Republic, it is in our interest to reassert Cicero's pertinence to politics in the twenty-first century, to re-establish Cicero's influence on contemporary philosophy and to restore Cicero's reputation as a role model for anyone who champions democracy over despotism. This is why Cicero still matters.

Notes

Introduction

1   The term 'dictator' we use today to refer to Hitler (Germany) or Pinochet (Chile) or Idi Amin (Uganda) or Kim Jong-Un (North Korea) comes from Ancient Rome. In times of crisis, for example, the threat of foreign invasion, the constitution of the Roman Republic allowed for one man to be granted absolute power, although the dictatorship was limited to six months. Julius Caesar used the military power under his control to force the Senate to grant him the dictatorship, and in February 44 BC Caesar was made dictator for life, *dictator in perpetuum*.

2   For an entertaining look at Cicero's presence in pop culture, see Lynn Fotheringham, 'Twentieth/twenty-first-century Cicero(s)', in Catherine Steel (ed.), *The Cambridge Companion to Cicero* (Cambridge: Cambridge University Press, 2013).

3   Maria Wyke (ed.), *Julius Caesar in Western Culture* (Malden, MA: Blackwell, 2006) is a collection of interdisciplinary and cross-cultural essays which explores the significance of Julius Caesar from the 50s BC through to the twenty-first century.

4   Ernst Badian, 'Julius Caesar', in S. Hornblower and A. Spawforth (eds.), *The Oxford Companion to Classical Civilization*, 2nd Edition (Oxford: Oxford University Press, 2014), 143.

5   See Mary Beard, *SPQR: A History of Ancient Rome* (New York: W.W. Norton, 2015).

6   Julius Caesar, *The Battle for Gaul, Book 4, 14-15* (Boston, MA: David R. Godine, 1980), 77.

7   Maria Wykes has written an important book on how throughout the twentieth-century America has perceived its role in the world through the image of Julius Caesar. See Maria Wyke, *Caesar in the USA* (Berkeley, CA: University of California Press, 2012).

8   On the scrolls found in Herculaneum, see Nicola Davis, 'Ancient Scrolls Charred by Vesuvius Could be Read Once Again', *The Guardian*, 3 October

2019, available online: https://www.theguardian.com/science/2019/oct/03/ancient-scrolls-charred-by-vesuvius-could-be-read-once-again

9   Attempts to argue that Cicero comes out well from Shakespeare's treatment of him are not convincing. See Yasunari Takada, 'Shakespeare's Cicero', in Mary Ann McGrail (ed.), *Shakespeare's Plutarch*, Special Issue of *Poetica: An International Journal of Linguistic-Literary Studies* 48 (Tokyo: Shubun International, 1997).

10   Camila Vergara, 'Populism as Plebeian Politics: Inequality, Domination, and Popular Empowerment', *The Journal of Political Philosophy*, Vol. 28, No. 2 (2020), 238.

11   Beard, *SPQR*, 281.

12   For a Left-wing interpretation of the Gracchus brothers, see Donald Busky, *Communism in History and Theory: From Utopian Socialism to the Fall of the Soviet Union* (Westport, CT: Greenwood Publishing Group, 2002), 27–31. Famously during the French Revolution, Francois-Noel Babeuf, the prominent Jacobin, adopted the pen name Gracchus Babeuf in their honour. For a more conservative interpretation, see Dylan Stevenson, 'The Brothers Gracchi: Reformers, Not Revolutionaries', *The Imaginative Conservative*, 19 November 2019, available online: https://theimaginativeconservative.org/2019/11/brothers-gracchi-reformers-not-revolutionaries-dylan-stevenson.html

13   'Cicero's Finest Hour' is the title of Ch. 1 of Mary Beard's masterful history of Rome, *SPQR*. The fact that this book, which covers the period from the foundation of Rome in 753 BC up to 192 AD, starts at 63 BC with Cicero is an indication of the pivotal role of Cicero in Roman history, even though Beard is not as charitable towards Cicero compared to some other scholars. On the Catilinarian conspiracy, see also Kathryn Tempest, *Cicero, Politics and Persuasion in Ancient Rome* (London: Bloomsbury 2011), 90–100, and Anthony Everitt, *Cicero: The Life and Times of Rome's Greatest Politician* (New York: Random House, 2003), 88–112.

14   See Jon Hall, 'Saviour of the Republic and Father of the Fatherland: Cicero and Political Crisis', in Catherine Steel (ed.) *The Cambridge Companion to Cicero*.

15   Tempest, *Cicero*, 86.

16   Miriam Griffin, (ed.), *A Companion to Julius Caesar* (Malden, Massachusetts, USA: Blackwell, 2008). See also Jan Nelis, 'Constructing

Fascist Identity: Benito Mussolini and the Myth of "Romanità", *The Classical World*, Vol. 100, No. 4 (2007), 391–415.

17 On fascism today, see Jason Stanley, *How Fascism Works: The Politics of Us and Them* (New York: Random House, 2018).

18 Gideon Rachman, *The Age of the Strongman: How the Cult of the Leader Threatens Democracy around the World* (London: Vintage, 2022).

19 Everything changed after the War when Oxford University introduced a degree programme in PPE (Philosophy, Politics and Economics). Today a very large number of UK politicians graduated in PPE from Oxford, including many prime ministers. Andy Beckett, 'PPE: The Oxford Degree that Runs Britain', *The Guardian*, 23 February 2017, available online: https://www.theguardian.com/education/2017/feb/23/ppe-oxford-university-degree-that-rules-britain

20 Beard, *SPQR*.

21 Tom Holland, *Rubicon* (London: Abacus, 2004). H. H. Scullard, *From the Gracchi to Nero* (London: Routledge, 1982).

22 Boris Johnson, *The Dream of Rome* (London: HarperCollins, 2006).

23 Klaus Bringmann, *A History of the Roman Republic* (Cambridge: Polity, 2007); David Shotter, *The Fall of the Roman Republic* (London: Routledge, 2005); Mary Beard and Michael Crawford, *Rome in the Late Republic* (London: Bloomsbury, 1999).

24 Katharina Volk, *The Roman Republic of Letters: Scholarship, Philosophy, and Politics in the Age of Cicero and Caesar* (Princeton: Princeton University Press, 2021).

25 Richard Alston, *Rome's Revolution: Death of the Republic & Birth of the Empire* (Oxford: Oxford University Press, 2015).

26 Everitt, *Cicero*; Tempest, *Cicero*; Elizabeth Rawson, *Cicero: A Portrait* (London: Allen Lane, 1975); David Shackleton Bailey, *Cicero* (London: Duckworth, 1971).

27 Thomas Mitchell, *Cicero the Senior Statesman* (New Haven, CT: Yale University Press, 1991); Christian Habicht, *Cicero the Politician* (Baltimore, MD: Johns Hopkins University Press, 1990).

28 Larry Diamond, 'Democracy's Arc: From Resurgent to Imperilled', *Journal of Democracy*, Vol. 33, No. 1 (January 2022), 163–79.

Chapter 1

1   For a very sophisticated account of *Homo Philosophicus* which has nothing to do with Cicero but focuses instead on the epistemology of self-knowledge, see Quassim Cassam, *Self-Knowledge for Humans* (Oxford: Oxford University Press, 2015), Ch.1 'Homo Philosophicus'.

2   Quoted in Lily Ross Taylor, *Party Politics in the Age of Caesar* (Berkeley: California University Press, 1949), 106.

3   Cicero, *Academic Questions, Treatise De Finibus, and Tusculan Disputations*, translated by C. D. Yonge (London: Henry G.Bohn, 1853), 338.

4   Cicero, *On Divination*, Book 2, 119.

5   Many intellectuals and academics are in grave danger, in many parts of the world. Scholars at Risk works to protect threatened scholars and promote academic freedom around the world. See www.scholarsatrisk.org.

6   Isaac Asimov, Column in *Newsweek*, 21 January 1980.

7   Everitt, *Cicero*, 254. Everitt also quotes Cicero: 'It was through my books that I was addressing the Senate and the people. I took the view that philosophy was a substitute for political activity', *On Divination*, Book 2, 7.

8   *Cicero's Letters to Atticus*, edited by D. R. Shakleton Bailey, Vol. 1 (Cambridge: Cambridge University Press, 1965), 211.

9   Gesine Manuwald. *Cicero* (London: I.B. Tauris 2015), 86.

10   See Ruth Morello, 'Further Voices and Familiar Perspectives in Cicero's Letters', *Hermathena*, Nos. 202–3, Summer-Winter 2017 (2022).

11   *Squid Game* is a South Korean television series from 2021 (Netflix's most-watched series) where cash-strapped contestants play a series of children's games in the hope of winning a multi-million prize. Participants who lost a game were killed.

12   On violence as a way of life in Republican Rome, see Andrew Lintott, *Violence in Republican Rome*, 2nd Edition (Oxford: Oxford University Press, 1999). On violence as a political tool during the Roman Republic, see also Alston, *Rome's Revolution*.

13   R.H. Barrow, *The Romans* (London: Penguin Books, 1949), 70.

14 Quoted in Anthony Corbeill, 'Cicero and the Intellectual Milieu of the Late Republic', in Catherine Steel (ed.), *The Cambridge Companion to Cicero*, 20.

15 Catherine Steel, *Reading Cicero: Genre and Performance in Late Republican Rome* (London: Duckworth, 2005), 137. See also Yelena Baraz, *A Written Republic: Cicero's Philosophical Politics* (Princeton: Princeton University Press, 2012), 9: 'He [Cicero] turned to writing as an additional arena for political activity.' See also Corbeill, 'Cicero and the Intellectual Milieu', 23: 'to Cicero the intellectual life is an important aspect of the political life'. Corbeill goes on to say that 'He [Cicero] never doubted that this two-fold activity constituted a single achievement, and that its rewards were preferable to the commercial successes of the businessman, the hermeticism of the scholar and the personal glory of military conquest', 24.

16 I'm paraphrasing Katharina Volk here. See *Roman Republic of Letters*, Ch. 3 'Engaged Philosophy', especially pp. 74–93.

17 Volk, *Roman Republic of Letters*, 8.

18 Baraz, *A Written Republic,* 11.

19 Raphael Woolf, *The Philosophy of a Roman Sceptic* (London: Routledge, 2015), 3 and 4.

20 Cicero, *On Obligations*, Book 1.13, translated by P. G. Walsh (Oxford: Oxford University Press, 2000), 7.

21 Cicero, *On Obligations,* Book 1.26, 10.

22 On the so-called 'Cato Wars' between Cicero and Caesar, see Volk, *Roman Republic of Letters*, 134–9.

23 See Peter Stothard, *Crassus: The First Tycoon* (New Haven, CT: Yale University Press, 2022).

24 Martha Nussbaum, 'Political Philosophy and International Feminism', in C. P. Ragland and S. Heidt (eds.), *What Is Philosophy?* (New Haven, CT: Yale University Press, 2001), 145.

25 Robert A. Kaster, 'Cicero Portraying Cicero', in Francesca Romana Berno and Giuseppe La Bua (eds.), *Portraying Cicero in Literature, Culture, and Politics: From Ancient to Modern Times* (Berlin: De Gruyter, 2022).

26 See Cary J. Nederman, *The Bonds of Humanity: Cicero's Legacies in European Social and Political Thought, ca. 1100–ca. 1550* (University Park: Pennsylvania State University Press, 2020).

27 Petrarch, *Old Grammarian*, in *Petrarch: The First Modern Scholar and Man of Letters*, by J. H. Robertson (London and New York: G.P. Putnam's Sons, 1898), 244. See also Tempest, *Cicero*, 122–4.

28 Quoted in Manuwald, *Cicero*, 150.

29 Quoted in Nicholas P. Cole, 'Nineteenth-century Ciceros', in Catherine Steel (ed.), *The Cambridge Companion to Cicero* (Cambridge: Cambridge University Press, 2013), 339.

30 Quoted in Manuwald, *Cicero*, 150–1.

31 Cole, 'Nineteenth-century Ciceros', 339.

32 I'm grateful to Ciaran Lynch for suggesting this terminology.

33 See 'Entrevista a Romano Mussolini: "Without My Father There Would Never Have Been Such a Thing as Fascism"', *HAOL*, Núm. 7 (Primavera, 2005), 112.

34 Philippe Rousselot, 'Cicéron face aux dictateurs, 1920–1945', in Francesca Romana Berno and Giuseppe La Bua (eds.), *Portraying Cicero in Literature, Culture, and Politics* (Berlin: De Gruyter, 2022).

35 Tim Elliott, 'America Is Eerily Retracing Rome's Steps to a Fall. Will It Turn Around before It's Too Late?' *Politico*, 11 March 2020, available online: https://www.politico.com/news/magazine/2020/11/03/donald-trump-julius-caesar-433956

36 Volk, *Roman Republic of Letters*.

37 On Brutus's *De Virtute* and its influence on Cicero, see Volk, *Roman Republic of Letters*, 115–16. On Brutus' life and thought, see Kathryn Tempest, *Brutus: The Noble Conspirator* (New Haven, CT: Yale University Press, 2017).

38 Plutarch, 'The Life of Caius Gracchus', in *Lives*, Vol. X (Cambridge, MA: Harvard University Press, 1989), 238.

39 Alston, *Rome's Revolution*, x. He goes on to explain: 'Food, money, and violence are the realities of power', xi.

40 J. P. V. D. Balsdon, 'Cicero the Man', in T. A. Dorey (ed.), *Cicero* (New York: Basic Books, 1965). Quoted in Robin Lane Fox, *The Classical World* (London: Penguin, 2006), 366.

41 Malcolm Schofield, *Cicero* (Oxford: Oxford University Press, 2021), 14.

Chapter 2

1   I have been told that there are political philosophers who teach Rawls's
     Political Liberalism (1993) or his *The Law of Peoples* (1999) but have never
     read his *A Theory of Justice* (1971). To me that's heresy, but as the saying
     goes, the world is beautiful because it is varied.

2   *On Obligations*, translated by P. D. Walsh (Oxford: Oxford University
     Press, 2000). *De Officiis* has also been translated, bizarrely, as 'The Offices'
     by Thomas Cockmas (first published, 1699), in *Cicero's Offices, Essays on
     Friendship & Old Age and Selected Letters* (London: J.M. Dent, 1909).

3   'Esta obra [*Sobre los Deberes*] en realdad es un complemento de sus
     tratados *De Republica* y *De Legibus* y el verdadero tratado de politica
     de Cicerón', José Guillén Cabañero, 'Introduction' to *Cicerón: Sobre Los
     Deberes* (Madrid: Alianza Editorial, 2001), 20.

4   Cicero, *De Officiis*, Book Three, 50, translated by Walter Miller, Loeb
     Classical Library (Cambridge, MA: Harvard University Press, 1968), 319.

5   Cicero, *Pro Marcello*, Par. 1, in *The Orations of Marcus Tullius Cicero*,
     translated by C. D. Yonge (London: George Bell & Sons, 1891). D. D. Dyer
     suggests that in this text Cicero issues a clear summons to tyrannicide, see
     his 'Rhetoric and Intention in Cicero's Pro Marcello', *The Journal of Roman
     Studies*, Vol. 80 (1990), 17–30.

6   Cicero, *De Officiis*, 15.

7   On post-truth, see Vittorio Bufacchi, 'Truth, Lies and Tweets: A Consensus
     Theory of Post-Truth', *Philosophy and Social Criticism*, Vol. 47, No. 3
     (2021), 347–61.

8   For a more detailed analysis of this point, see Maria Paola Ferretti, *The
     Public Perspective: Public Justification and the Ethics of Belief* (London:
     Rowan and Littlefield, 2018).

9   Alan Ryan, *On Politics: A History of Political Thought from Herodotus to the
     Present* (London: Allen Lane, 2012), 145.

10   Cheryl Misak, *Pragmatism and Deliberation* (London: Routledge, 2000).

11   *The Academics of Cicero*, translated by James S. Reid (London: Macmillan,
     1880), 33.

12   *The Academics of Cicero*, 33.

13 quoted in Manuwald, *Cicero*, 102.

14 Walter Nicgorski, *Cicero's Skepticism and His Recovery of Political Philosophy* (New York: Palgrave, 2016), 18–19.

15 Nicgorski, *Cicero's Skepticism*, 7.

16 Cicero, *On Duties*, Book 1, in *Cicero: On Living and Dying Well*, translated by Thomas Habinek (London: Penguin Books, 2012), 116–17.

17 On trust see Russell Hardin, *Trust and Trustworthiness* (New York: Sage, 2002).

18 This is the main message of Onora O'Neill's 2002 Reith Lectures: *A Question of Trust: The BBC Reith Lectures 2002* (Cambridge: Cambridge University Press, 2002).

19 Thomas Hobbes, *Leviathan*, Book 1, Ch.13 (London: Penguin, 1968), 186.

20 For an account of how Cicero's *On Duties* became very relevant again in the United States in recent years, see Danielle Allen, 'Cicero used to be boring. With Trump around, he's breathtaking', *The Washington Post*, 4 January 2017.

21 Schofield, *Cicero*, 67. On the difficulty of translating the term *ius*, see also Elizabeth Asmis, 'The State as a Partnership: Cicero's Definition of Res Publica in His Work on the State', *History of Political Thought*, Vol. 25 (2004), 569–98.

22 'Justice – the justice inherent in a legal order, if upheld by the government system – binds human beings together, and makes them into an association: a community'. Schofield, *Cicero*, 68.

23 On Rawls's two theories of justice, see Brian Barry, *Theories of Justice* (Berkeley, CA: California University Press, 1991).

24 See Daniel Kapust, 'Thomas Hobbes, Cicero, and the Road Not Taken', in Daniel Kapust and Gary Remer (eds.), *The Ciceronian Tradition in Political Theory* (Madison: The University of Wisconsin Press, 2021).

25 Jill Harries, 'The Law in Cicero's Writings', in C. Steel (ed.), *The Cambridge Companion to Cicero*, 120.

26 Cicero, *De Officiis,* Book One, 20, 22–3, emphasis added.

27 There are a few notable exceptions, including Judith Shklar, *The Faces of Injustice* (New Haven, CT: Yale University Press, 1990); Iris Marion Young, *Justice and the Politics of Difference* (Princeton, NJ: Princeton University Press, 1990); Nancy Fraser, 'On Justice', *New Left Review*, Vol. 74, March-

April 2012; Eric Heinze, *The Concept of Injustice* (London: Routledge, 2013); and Vittorio Bufacchi, *Social Injustice: Essays in Political Philosophy* (London: Palgrave, 2012).

28   Cicero, *De Officiis*, Book One, 24, 25.

29   Cicero, *On Duties*, in *On Living and Dying Well*, 117

30   Cicero, *De Officiis*, Book One, 25, 27.

31   Cicero, *De Officiis,* Book One, 26, 27.

32   Cicero, *De Officiis,* Book One, 26, 27

33   Cicero, *De Officiis,* Book One, 44, 49.

34   Cicero, *De Officiis,* Book One, 23, 25.

35   Judith Shklar, *The Faces of Injustice*, 41.

36   Cicero, *De Officiis*, Book Three, 21, 289.

Chapter 3

1   See Vittorio Bufacchi, 'Liberalism and Structural Injustice: When the Solution Becomes the Problem', in Duncan Ivison (ed.), *Research Handbook on Liberalism* (Cheltenham: Edward Elgar, forthcoming).

2   Iseult Honohan, *Civic Republicanism* (London: Routledge, 2002), 1.

3   Cicero, *The Republic*, Book 1: par. 39, in *Cicero: The Republic and the Laws*, translated by Niall Rudd (Oxford: Oxford University Press, 2008), 19. The influence of Aristotle on Cicero is clearly evident here.

4   Honohan, *Civic Republicanism*, 1.

5   See Norberto Bobbio, *The Future of Democracy* (Cambridge: Polity, 1987), 106.

6   See Onora O'Neill, 'The Dark Side of Human Rights', *International Affairs*, Vol. 81, No. 2 (2005), 427–39.

7   Stephen Medcalf, 'Neoliberalism: The Idea That Swallowed the World', *The Guardian*, 18 August 2017, available online: https://www.theguardian.com/news/2017/aug/18/neoliberalism-the-idea-that-changed-the-world

8 See Brian Barry, 'The Public Interest', in Anthony Quinton (ed.), *Political Philosophy* (Oxford: Oxford University Press, 1967).

9 For a more detailed account of the death of Lucretia, see Michael Grant, *Roman Myths* (London: Penguin, 1973), 189. Mary Beard's Gifford Lectures, delivered at the University of Edinburgh in 2019, Lecture 3: Lucretia and the Politics of Sexual Violence, is available online:https://giffordsedinburgh.com/2019/05/09/lecture-3-lucretia-and-the-politics-of-sexual-violence/

10 See Melissa Lane, *Greek and Roman Political Ideas* (London: Penguin, 2014), 184.

11 Cicero, *The Republic*, Book 1: par. 46, in *Cicero: The Republic and the Laws*, 21.

12 See Richard Bellamy, *Citizenship: A Very Short Introduction* (Oxford: Oxford University Press, 2008).

13 See Jed Atkins, *Roman Political Thought* (Cambridge: Cambridge University Press, 2018), 65.

14 On how to measure freedom, see Ian Carter, *A Measure of Freedom* (Oxford: Oxford University Press, 1999).

15 Hillel Steiner, *An Essay on Rights* (Oxford: Blackwell, 1994).

16 Philip Pettit, *Republicanism: A Theory of Freedom and Government* (Oxford: Oxford University Press, 1997).

17 Donald R. Dudley, *The Romans: 850 BC – 337 AD* (New York: Barnes and Nobles Books, 1993).

18 See Susan Treggiari, 'Consent to Marriage: Some Aspects of Law and Reality', *Echos du Monde Classique/Classical Views*, Vol. 26, No. 1 (1982), 34–44.

19 These speeches are known as *In Verrem*, see Cicero, *The Verrine Orations*, Vols. 1 and 2, Loeb Classical Library (Cambridge, MA: Harvard University Press, 1989).

20 Pettit, *Republicanism*, 52. See also Frank Lovett, *A General Theory of Domination and Justice* (Oxford: Oxford University Press, 2010), who points out that social power is arbitrary 'to the extent that its potential exercise is not externally constrained by effective rules, procedures, or goals that are common knowledge of all persons or groups concerned', 96.

21 Of course there are those who defend Caesar, and insist on his great virtues. See David Konstan, 'Clemency as a Virtue', *Classical Philology*, Vol. 100, No. 4 (October 2005), 337–46.

22 Cicero, *The Republic and the Laws*, 20.

23 Taylor, *Party Politics in the Age of Caesar*, 164.

24 Alston, *Rome's Revolution*, 142.

25 Ann Vasaly highlights Cicero's judicial speeches, including the prosecution of Verres, to stress the importance of Cicero's oratory in the accumulation of the political capital vital to his political career, see Ann Vasaly, 'The Political Impact of Cicero's Speeches', in Catherine Steel (ed.), *The Cambridge Companion to Cicero*.

26 For a more detailed analysis of the mixed constitution in Cicero's *On the Republic*, see James Zetzel, 'Political Philosophy', in Catherine Steel (ed.), *Cambridge Companion to Cicero*; Neal Wood, *Cicero's Social and Political Thought* (Berkeley, CA: University of California Press, 1991); Schofield, *Cicero*.

27 Cicero, *The Republic*, Book 1: par. 43, in *Cicero: The Republic and the Laws*, 20.

28 Ibid., 21.

29 Ibid., 30.

30 On this issue see Honohan, *Civic Republicanism*, 30–41.

31 Maurizio Viroli credits Cicero for helping to define the classical theory of the 'res publica'; see his *Republicanism* (New York: Hill and Wang, 1999).

32 See also Francesca Nenci, 'Introduzione', in *Cicerone: La Repubblica* (Milan: Rizzoli, 2008), 64–8.

33 For an excellent analysis of *res publica* and *res populi*, see Schofield, *Cicero*, 47–9.

34 See Schofield, *Cicero*, 57, n60. See also E. Fantham, '*Aequabilitas* in Cicero's Political Theory and the Greek Tradition of Proportional Justice', *Classical Quarterly*, Vol. 23 (1973), 285–90.

35 Book II, 23: Cicero, *On the Nature of the Gods*, Loeb Classical Library (Cambridge, MA: Harvard University Press, 1933).

36 Cicero, *The Republic*, Book 1: par. 69, in *Cicero: The Republic and the Laws*, 32.

37 Ibid., 22–3.

38 Cicero, *The Republic*, Book 1: par. 51, in *Cicero: The Republic and the Laws*, 24.

39 See John W. Maynor, *Republicanism in the Modern World* (Cambridge: Polity, 2003).

Chapter 4

1   Apart from Plato and Aristotle, friendship is the subject of an 'essay' by Michel de Montaigne, and the subject of enquiry by Aquinas, Kant, Kierkegaard, Ralph Waldo Emerson, Nietzsche, and Iris Murdoch amongst others. For an overview of philosophers on friendship, see Mark Vernon, *The Philosophy of Friendship* (Basingstoke: Palgrave, 2005).

2   Quoted in Manuwald, *Cicero*, 117–18.

3   In *Tusculan Disputations*, in Book 2 'On Bearing Pain', Book 3 'On Grief of Mind', and Book 4 'On Other Perturbations of the Mind', Cicero makes extensive use of poetry.

4   For a short but more technical analysis of love in Plato, see F. C. White, 'Love and Beauty in Plato's Symposium', *The Journal of Hellenic Studies*, Vol. 109 (1989), 149–57.

5   Aristotle's analysis of friendship can be found in his *Nicomachean Ethics*, edited by Sarah Broadie and Christopher Rowe (Oxford: Oxford University Press, 2002).

6   Cicero, 'On Friendship', in *Cicero: On Living and Dying Well,* 85.

7   Ibid., 87.

8   Ibid., 85–6.

9   Ibid., 86.

10   Cicero, 'Philippic II', in *Cicero: Political Speeches*, translated by D. H. Berry (Oxford: Oxford University Press, 2006), 231.

11   Ibid., 244–5.

12   Cicero, 'On Friendship', 81–2, emphasis added.

13   Ibid., 102.

14   Ibid.

15   Jean-Jacques Rousseau, *Reveries of the Solitary Walker* (Oxford: Oxford University Press, 2011).

16   Cicero, 'On Friendship', 85. The Latin reads: *Amor enim, ex quo amicitia nominata est.*

17   Ibid., 87.

18 Ibid., 93.

19 Ibid., 96.

20 On 'political friendship', and in particular how the term *amicitia* relates to and overlaps with the concepts of *fides* (trust) and *factio* (partisanship), see Rachel Feig Vishnia, *Roman Elections in the Age of Cicero* (London: Routledge, 2012), 116–17.

21 Cicero, 'On Friendship', 93.

22 Ibid., 97.

23 Ibid., 98.

24 Accounts of equality in Cicero's political thought are very rare. Schofield, *Cicero*, is an exception to the rule.

25 This is more significant than it may seem. As Volk points put: 'the joined *studia* [communal intellectual engagements] were – and were perceived to be – an important manifestation of the friendship of Roman upperclass men', Volk, *Roman Republic of Letters*, 47.

26 On the role of emotions in Cicero's philosophy, see Katharina Volk 'Should You Be Upset? Cicero on the Desirability of Emotion', *Antigone*, available online: https://antigonejournal.com/2022/01/cicero-emotion/

27 Judith Shklar, *On Political Obligation* (New Haven, CT: Yale University Press, 2019). See also Volk, *Roman Republic of Letters*, 176.

28 Craig Condella, 'Why Can't We Be Virtual Friends?' in D. E. Wittkower (ed.), *Facebook and Philosophy* (Chicago, IL: Open Court, 2010). By 2019 this number went up to 338, see https://www.brandwatch.com/blog/facebook-statistics/

29 Philip Freeman, 'Introduction', in *How To Be a Friend: An Ancient Guide to True Friendship*, by Cicero, translated by Philip Freeman (Princeton: Princeton University Press, 2018).

30 On freedom of speech and its limits, see Suzanne Whitten, *A Republican Theory of Free Speech* (London: Palgrave, 2021).

31 Casey Newton, 'Mark in the Metaverse', *The Verge*, 22 July 2021, available online: https://www.theverge.com/22588022/mark-zuckerberg-facebook-ceo-metaverse-interview

32 Robert Nozick, *Anarchy, State, Utopia* (Oxford: Blackwell, 1974).

Chapter 5

1   These statistics are taken from United Nations, Department of Economic
    and Social Affairs, Population Division (2017). World Population Ageing
    2017 – Highlights (ST/ESA/SER.A/397).

2   See Vittorio Bufacchi, *Everything Must Change: Philosophical Lessons from
    Lockdown* (Manchester: Manchester University Press, 2021), Ch. 3, 'Old
    Age in the Time of Coronavirus'.

3   Christine Overall, 'How Old Is Old? Changing Conceptions of Old Age', in
    G. Scarre (ed.), *The Palgrave Handbook of the Philosophy of Aging* (London:
    Palgrave, 2016), 15.

4   Ibid., 24.

5   This is the position advocated by the charity Age Concern, see https://
    www.ageaction.ie/how-we-can-help/campaigning-policy/human-
    rights-and-older-people. The UN Office of the High Commissioner for
    Human Rights takes a similar position:https://www.ohchr.org/EN/Issues/
    OlderPersons/Pages/OlderPersonsIndex.aspx.

6   Cicero, 'On Old Age', in Michael Grant (trans.), *Cicero: Selected Works*
    (London: Penguin, 1971), 238.

7   Ibid., 223.

8   Ibid., 220.

9   Ibid., 226.

10 Ibid., 216.

11 Ibid., 229.

12 Quoted in Audrey Anton, 'Aging in Classical Philosophy', in G. Scarre
    (ed.), *The Palgrave Handbook of the Philosophy of Aging* (London: Palgrave,
    2016), 130. Audrey also reminds us that in his *On the Shortness of Life*
    Seneca makes a similar point, warning us that the pursuit of desires
    interferes with our higher, more noble pursuits.

13 Cicero, 'On Old Age', 240.

14 Norberto Bobbio, *Old Age and Other Essays* (London: Polity, 2001). Bobbio
    wrote his essay 'Old Age' when he was eighty-five years old, Cicero wrote
    'On Old Age' when he was sixty-two years old.

15 https://www.theguardian.com/commentisfree/2019/nov/15/labour-free-broadband-digital-future-public.

16 See H. J. McCloskey, 'Rights – Some Conceptual Issues', *Australasian Journal of Philosophy*, Vol. 54, No. 2 (August 1976).

17 Cicero, 'On Old Age', 216.

18 Ibid., 238.

19 Anton, 'Aging in Classical Philosophy', 121.

20 Jeanette McClellan, 'Benefits of a Gardening Project for People with Dementia in Nursing Homes', *Nursing Times* [online], Vol. 114, No. 2 (2018), 38–40, available online: https://www.nursingtimes.net/roles/care-home-nurses/benefits-of-a-gardening-project-for-people-with-dementia-in-nursing-homes-15-01-2018/.

21 Cicero, 'On Old Age', 237.

Chapter 6

1 A. Trevor Hodge, *Roman Aqueducts and Water Supply*, 2nd Edition (London: Duckworth, 2002).

2 Melissa Lane, *Greek and Roman Political Ideas* (London: Pelican, 2014), 3.

3 Sabine MacCormack, 'Cicero in Late Antiquity', in Catherine Steel (ed.), *Cambridge Companion to Cicero*, 251: 'The very stones of Rome spoke of Cicero's linguistic finesse and his personality.'

4 Wood, *Cicero's Social and Political Thought*.

5 Quoted in Michael Parenti, *The Assassination of Julius Caesar: A People's History of Ancient Rome* (New York: The New Press, 2003), 86.

6 Gary Remer also strongly believes that Cicero's political thought is still relevant today, and his communitarian ideas of democratic deliberation and political morality are pertinent to modern debates in contemporary political philosophy; see Gary Remer, *Ethics and the Orator: The Ciceronian Tradition of Political Morality* (Chicago: University of Chicago Press, 2017). See also Daniel Kapust and Gary Remer (eds.), *The Ciceronian Tradition in Political Theory* (Madison, WI: University of Wisconsin Press, 2021).

7   These are the key findings of the 'The Global State of Democracy Report 2021: Building Resilience in a Pandemic Era', published on 22 November 2021 by the International Institute for Democracy and Electoral Assistance, an intergovernmental organization based in Stockholm. https://www.idea.int/news-media/news/democracy-faces-perfect-storm-world-becomes-more-authoritarian. See here for the full Report: https://www.idea.int/gsod/sites/default/files/2021-11/the-global-state-of-democracy-2021_1.pdf

8   Quoted in Bringmann, *A History of the Roman Republic*, 294.

9   Volk, *The Roman Republic of Letters*, 178. One of the premises of Volk's important book is the belief that the scholarship and the political system during Cicero's time were interdepended, since the intellectual activity 'was wholly embedded within the actual *res publica*, the Republican political system run by the same men who also engaged in scholarship', 22.

10   Raphael Woolf, *Cicero: The Philosophy of a Roman Sceptic* (London: Routledge, 2015), 127.

11   Wood, *Cicero's Social and Political Thought*, 120–1.

12   Cicero, *De Natura Deorum* (On the Nature of the Gods), Book 2, xxix, quoted in Anthony Trollope, *The Life of Cicero*, Vol. 2 (London: The Trollope Society, [1880] 1993), 359–60.

13   Zvi Yavetz, 'Cicero: A Man of Letters in Politics', in Gillian Clark and Tessa Rajak (eds.), *Philosophy and Power in the Greco-Roman World* (Oxford: Oxford University Press, 2002), 177.

14   Woolf, *Cicero*, 67. Woolf is referring to one of Cicero's less well-known works, *On Fate*.

15   Umberto Eco, *The Name of the Rose* (Boston: Houghton Mifflin Harcourt, 2012), 120.

16   Cicero, *De Inventione*, Loeb Classical Library (Cambridge, MA: Harvard University Press, 1949), 5.

17   Wood, *Cicero's Social & Political Thought*, 91.

18   Ibid., 96–7.

19   Alston, *Rome's Revolution*, xi, emphasis added. Alston goes on to say: 'Politics is not just, or even primarily, about great ideas and debates, the dramas of the great men and their conflicts and ideas. Men and women may trade in ideas, but to live they need material: food and fuel and clothes and shelter', Alston, *Rome's Revolution*, xi.

20   Alston, *Rome's Revolution*, 124, is very good on this.

21   Johnson, *The Dream of Rome*, 65, emphasis added. Johnson was UK Prime Minister from 2019 to 2022.

22   Alston, *Rome's Revolution*, 17.

23   Amanda Wilcox, 'Cicero the satirist? Scurrilous poses in the *Letters*', *Hermathena*, Nos. 202–203 (Summer-Winter 2017 [2022]).

24   Taylor, *Party Politics in the Age of Caesar*, 3.

25   Micheal Fontaine, Foreword to *How to Tell a Joke: An Ancient Guide to the Art of Humour* (Princeton: Princeton University Press, 2021).

26   From Plutarch, *Fall of the Roman Republic, Six Lives*, translated by Rex Warner (London: Penguin Classics, 1958), 299.

27   Quoted in Susan Treggiari, *Terentia, Tullia and Publilia: The Women of Cicero's Family* (London: Routledge, 2007), 134.

28   Treggiari, *Terentia, Tullia and Publilia*, 141.

29   See Barbara Del Giovane, 'Da iocosus a consularis scurra. Rappresentazioni del Cicerone Umorista', in Francesca Romana Berno and Giuseppe La Bua (eds.), *Portraying Cicero in Literature, Culture, and Politics* (Berlin: De Gruyter, 2022).

30   On Tito and Cicero's jokes, see https://insidestory.org.au/funny-things-happen-on-the-way-to-the-forum/. On Cicero's wit, see also Francis W. Kelsey, 'Cicero as a Wit', *The Classical Journal*, Vol. 3, No. 1 (November 1907), 3–10.

31   This is Anthony Trollope's translation: 'In English, if meaning the latter [elevated to the gallows], we should say that such a man must be "put out of the way"'. In other words, 'Let us reward him, but for the moment let us be rid of him'. Trollope, *The Life of Cicero*, Vol. 2, 282.

32   Tempest, *Cicero*, 204.

33   Charles Nauert Jr., *Humanism and the Culture of Renaissance Europe*, 2nd Edition (Cambridge, UK: Cambridge University Press, 2006). See also David Marsh, 'Cicero in the Renaissance', in Catherine Steel (ed.), *The Cambridge Companion to Cicero*, 316: 'Cicero's influence on the Renaissance is central to the movement we call humanism.'

34   On Cicero's influence on these authors, and many others, see Michael Hawley, *Natural Law Republicanism: Cicero's Liberal Legacy* (Oxford: Oxford University Press, 2022).

35 Matthew Fox, 'Cicero During the Enlightenment', in Catherine Steel (ed.), *The Cambridge Companion to Cicero*, 319. On the influence of Cicero on Montesquieu, see Igor Moraes Santos 'Montesquieu on Cicero. Historiographical, political, and philosophical dimensions of a modern portrait', in Francesca Romana Berno and Giuseppe La Bua (eds.), *Portraying Cicero in Literature, Culture, and Politics*. On Cicero and Kant see Manfred Khun, 'Kant and Cicero', in Volker Gerhardt, Rolf-Peter Horstmann and Ralph Schumacher (eds.), *Kant und die Berliner Aufklärung: Akten des IX. Internationalen Kant-Kongresses* (Berlin: De Gruyter, 2001). On Cicero and John Adams see Meyer Reinhold, 'The Influence of Cicero on John Adams', *Ciceroniana on Line: A Journal of Roman Thought*, Vol. 8 (2015), available online: https://www.ojs.unito.it/index.php/COL/article/view/1278/1114.

36 In Latin, '*quasi natura et genere disiuncti sint*', quoted in Taylor, *Party Politics in the Age of Caesar*, 106.

Epilogue

1 The literature on this topic is immense, but see Serena Parekh, *No Refuge: Ethics and the Global Refugee Crisis* (Oxford: Oxford University Press, 2020), and David Owen, *What Do We Owe to Refugees?* (Cambridge: Polity, 2020).

2 From a speech delivered in 56 BC, quoted in Katheryn Tempest, *Cicero*, 13.

3 For a strong argument on the cosmopolitan dimension in Cicero's ethics, see Schofield, *Cicero*, Ch.4 'Cosmopolitanism, Imperialism, and the Idea of Law', 105–46.

4 Catherine Tracy, 'The People's Consul: The Significance of Cicero's Use of the Term "Popularis"', *Illinois Classical Studies*, No. 33–34 (2008–2009), 181–99.

5 Cicero, *The Republic and the Laws*, 17.

6 Cicero, *The Republic and the Laws*, 158: The Laws, III, 20.

7 Cicero, *Letters to Atticus*, 2.19, between 7 and 14 July 59 BC, quoted in Robin Lane Fox, *The Classical World*, 377.

8   Cicero, 'On the Agrarian Law', 2.6–7, quoted in Kathryn Tempest, *Cicero*, 88.

9   Quoted in Tempest, *Cicero*, 109.

10 See Vishnia, *Roman Elections in the Age of Cicero*.

11 Stothard, *Crassus*, 143–4.

12 For an original analysis of the wrongness of corruption, see Emanuela Ceva, 'Political Corruption as a Relational Injustice', *Social Philosophy and Policy*, Vol. 35, No. 2 (2018), 118–37. See also Emanuela Ceva and Maria Paola Ferretti, *Political Corruption: The Internal Enemy of Public Institutions* (New York: Oxford University Press, 2021).

13 Adam Przeworski, *Democracy and the Market: Political and Economic Reforms in Eastern Europe and Latin America* (Cambridge: Cambridge University Press, 1991).

14 Cicero, *On Duties*, Book 1, in *Cicero: On Living and Dying Well*, 116.

15 Ibid., 114.

16 Quintus Tullius Cicero, *How to Win an Election: An Ancient Guide for Modern Politicians* (Princeton: Princeton University Press, 2012).

17 Hannah Arendt, 'Truth and Politics', in Peter Baehr (ed.), *The Portable Hannah Arendt* (London: Penguin, 2000).

18 Maria Paola Ferretti argues that citizens are responsible for the way they participate in political communication and debate, including the truthfulness of information they post or disseminate on social media. See Maria Paola Ferretti, 'Fake News and the Responsibilities of Citizens', *Social Theory and Practice*, Vol. 49, No. 4 (October 2023).

19 Cicero, *The Laws*, Book 1, in *Cicero: The Republic and The Laws*, 107.

Bibliography

Alston, Richard. *Rome's Revolution: Death of the Republic & Birth of the Empire*, Oxford: Oxford University Press 2015.

Anton, Audrey. 'Aging in Classical Philosophy', in G. Scarre (ed.), *The Palgrave Handbook of the Philosophy of Aging*, London: Palgrave 2016.

Arendt, Hannah. 'Truth and Politics', in Peter Baehr (ed.), *The Portable Hannah Arendt*, London: Penguin 2000.

Aristotle. *Nicomachean Ethics*, edited by Sarah Broadie and Christopher Rowe, Oxford: Oxford University Press 2002.

Asmis, Elizabeth. 'The State as a Partnership: Cicero's Definition of Res Publica in his Work on the State', *History of Political Thought*, Vol. 25, 2004.

Atkins, Jed. *Roman Political Thought*, Cambridge: Cambridge University Press 2018.

Badian, Ernst. 'Julius Caesar', in Simon Hornblower and Antony Spawforth (eds.), *The Oxford Companion to Classical Civilization*, 2nd Edition, Oxford: Oxford University Press 2014.

Baraz, Yelena. *A Written Republic: Cicero's Philosophical Politics*, Princeton: Princeton University Press 2012.

Barrow, R. H. *The Romans*, London: Penguin Books 1949.

Barry, Brian. 'The Public Interest', in Anthony Quinton (ed.), *Political Philosophy*, Oxford: Oxford University Press 1967.

Barry, Brian. *Theories of Justice*, Berkeley, CA: California University Press 1991.

Beard, Mary. *SPQR: A History of Ancient Rome*, New York: W.W. Norton 2015.

Beard, Mary and Michael Crawford. *Rome in the Late Republic*, London: Bloomsbury 1999.

Bellamy, Richard. *Citizenship: A Very Short Introduction*, Oxford: Oxford University Press 2008.

Bobbio, Norberto. *The Future of Democracy*, Cambridge: Polity 1987.

Bobbio, Norberto. *Old Age and Other Essays*, London: Polity 2001.

Bringmann, Klaus. *A History of the Roman Republic*, Cambridge: Polity 2007.

Bufacchi, Vittorio. *Social Injustice: Essays in Political Philosophy*, London: Palgrave 2012.

Bufacchi, Vittorio. 'Truth, Lies and Tweets: A Consensus Theory of Post-Truth', *Philosophy and Social Criticism*, Vol. 47, No. 3, 2021.

Bufacchi, Vittorio. *Everything Must Change: Philosophical Lessons from Lockdown*, Manchester: Manchester University Press 2021.

Bufacchi, Vittorio. 'Liberalism and Structural Injustice: When the Solution Becomes the Problem', in Duncan Ivison (ed.), *Research Handbook on Liberalism*, Cheltenham: Edward Elgar forthcoming.

Busky, Donald. *Communism in History and Theory: From Utopian Socialism to the Fall of the Soviet Union*, Westport, CT: Greenwood Publishing Group 2002.

Cabañero, José Guillén. 'Introducción', *Cicerón: Sobre Los Deberes*, Madrid: Alianza Editorial 2001.

Caesar, Julius. *The Battle of Gaul*, translated by Anne and Peter Wiseman, Boston, MA: David R. Godinee 1980.

Carter, Ian. *A Measure of Freedom*, Oxford: Oxford University Press 1999.

Ceva, Emanuela. 'Political Corruption as a Relational Injustice', *Social Philosophy and Policy*, Vol. 35, No. 2, 2018.

Ceva, Emanuela and Maria Paola Ferretti. *Political Corruption: The Internal Enemy of Public Institutions*, New York: Oxford University Press 2021.

Cicero, Marcus Tullius. *Tusculan Disputations*, in *Cicero, Academic Questions, Treatise De Finibus, and Tusculan Disputations*, translated by C. D. Yonge, London: Henry G. Bohn, 1853.

Cicero, Marcus Tullius. *The Academics of Cicero*, translated by James S. Reid, London: Macmillan 1880.

Cicero, Marcus Tullius. 'Pro Marcello', Par. 1, in C. D. Yonge (trans.), *The Orations of Marcus Tullius Cicero*, London: George Bell & Sons 1891.

Cicero, Marcus Tullius. *On the Nature of the Gods*, Loeb Classical Library, Cambridge, MA: Harvard University Press 1933.

Cicero, Marcus Tullius. *De Inventione*, Loeb Classical Library, Cambridge, MA: Harvard University Press, 1949.

Cicero, Marcus Tullius. *Cicero's Letters to Atticus*, edited by D. R. Shakleton Bailey, Vol. 1, Cambridge: Cambridge University Press, 1965.

Cicero, Marcus Tullius. *De Officiis*, translated by Walter Miller, Loeb Classical Library, Cambridge, MA: Harvard University Press, 1968.

Cicero, Marcus Tullius. 'On Old Age', in Michael Grant (trans.), *Cicero: Selected Works*, London: Penguin 1971.

Cicero, Marcus Tullius. *The Verrine Orations*, Vols.1 and 2, Loeb Classical Library, Cambridge, MA: Harvard University Press 1989.

Cicero, Marcus Tullius. *On Obligations*, translated by P. G. Walsh, Oxford: Oxford University Press 2000.

Cicero, Marcus Tullius. 'Philippic II', in D. H. Berry (trans.), *Cicero: Political Speeches*, Oxford: Oxford University Press 2006.

Cicero, Marcus Tullius. *Cicero: The Republic and the Laws*, translated by Niall Rudd, Oxford: Oxford University Press 2008.

Cicero, Marcus Tullius. 'On Duties', in Thomas Habinek (trans.), *Cicero: On Living and Dying Well*, London: Penguin Books 2012.

Cicero, Marcus Tullius. *How to Be a Friend: An Ancient Guide to True Friendship*, translated by Philip Freeman, Princeton: Princeton University Press 2018.

Cicero, Marcus Tullius. *How to Tell a Joke: An Ancient Guide to the Art of Humor*, translated by Michael Fontaine, Princeton: Princeton University Press 2021.

Cicero, Quintus Tullius. *How to Win an Election: An Ancient Guide for Modern Politicians*, Princeton: Princeton University Press 2012.

Cole, Nicholas P. 'Nineteenth-Century Ciceros', in Catherine Steel (ed.), *The Cambridge Companion to Cicero*, Cambridge: Cambridge University Press 2013.

Condella, Craig. 'Why Can't We Be Virtual Friends?', in D. E. Wittkower (ed.), *Facebook and Philosophy*, Chicago, IL: Open Court 2010.

Corbeill, Anthony. 'Cicero and the Intellectual Milieu of the Late Republic', in Catherine Steel (ed.), *The Cambridge Companion to Cicero*, Cambridge: Cambridge University Press 2013.

Del Giovane, Barbara. 'Da iocosus a consularis scurra. Rappresentazioni del Cicerone Umorista', in Francesca Romana Berno and Giuseppe La Bua (eds.), *Portraying Cicero in Literature, Culture, and Politics*, Berlin: De Gruyter 2022.

Diamond, Larry. 'Democracy's Arc: From Resurgent to Imperilled', *Journal of Democracy*, Vol. 33, No. 1, January 2022.

Dudley, Donald. *The Romans: 850 BC – 337 AD*, New York: Barnes and Nobles Books 1993.

Dyer, D. D. 'Rhetoric and Intention in Cicero's Pro Marcellum', *The Journal of Roman Studies*, Vol. 80, 1990.

Eco, Umberto. *The Name of the Rose*, Boston: Houghton Mifflin Harcourt 2012.

Everitt, Anthony. *Cicero: The Life and Times of Rome's Greatest Politician*, New York: Random House 2003.

Fantham, E. 'Aequabilitas in Cicero's Political Theory and the Greek Tradition of Proportional Justice', *Classical Quarterly*, Vol. 23, 1973.

Ferretti, Maria Paola. *The Public Perspective: Public Justification and the Ethics of Belief*, London: Rowan and Littlefield 2018.

Ferretti, Maria Paola. 'Fake News and the Responsibilities of Citizens', *Social Theory and Practice*, Vol. 49, No. 4, October 2023.

Fotheringham, Lynn. 'Twentieth/twenty-First-Century Cicero(s)', in Catherine Steel (ed.), *The Cambridge Companion to Cicero*, Cambridge: Cambridge University Press 2013.

Fox, Matthew. 'Cicero during the Enlightenment', in Catherine Steel (ed.), *The Cambridge Companion to Cicero*, Cambridge: Cambridge University Press 2013.

Fraser, Nancy. 'On Justice', *New Left Review*, Vol. 74, March-April 2012.

Freeman, Philip. 'Introduction', in Cicero, Philip Freeman (trans.), *How to Be a Friend: An Ancient Guide to True Friendship*, Princeton: Princeton University Press 2018.

Grant, Michael. *Roman Myths*, London: Penguin 1973.

Griffin, Miriam. *A Companion to Julius Caesar*. Malden, MA: Blackwell 2008.

Habicht, Christian. *Cicero the Politician*, Baltimore, MD: Johns Hopkins University Press 1990.

Hall, Jon. 'Saviour of the Republic and Father of the Fatherland: Cicero and Political Crisis', in C. Steel (ed.), *The Cambridge Companion to Cicero*, Cambridge: Cambridge University Press 2013.

Hardin, Russell. *Trust and Trustworthiness*, New York: Sage 2002.

Hawley, Michael. *Natural Law Republicanism: Cicero's Liberal Legacy*, Oxford: Oxford University Press 2022.

Heinze, Eric. *The Concept of Injustice*. Abington: Routledge 2013.

Hobbes, Thomas. *Leviathan*, London: Penguin 1968.

Hodge, A. Trevor. *Roman Aqueducts and Water Supply*, 2nd Edition, London: Duckworth 2002.

Holland, Tom. *Rubicon: The Triumph and Tragedy of the Roman Republic*, London: Abacus 2004.

Honohan, Iseult. *Civic Republicanism*, London: Routledge 2002.

Johnson, Boris. *The Dream of Rome*, London: HarperCollins 2006.

Kapust, Daniel and Gary Remer (eds.), *The Ciceronian Tradition in Political Theory*, Madison: University of Wisconsin Press 2021.

Kelsey, Francis W. 'Cicero as a Wit', *The Classical Journal*, Vol. 3, No. 1, November 1907.

Khun, Manfred. 'Kant and Cicero', in Volker Gerhardt, Rolf-Peter Horstmann and Ralph Schumacher (eds.), *Kant und die Berliner Aufklärung: Akten des IX. Internationalen Kant-Kongresses*, Berlin: De Gruyter 2001.

Konstan, David. 'Clemency as a Virtue', *Classical Philology*, Vol. 100, No. 4, October 2005.

Lane, Melissa. *Greek and Roman Political Ideas*, London: Penguin 2014.

Lane Fox, Robin. *The Classical World*, London: Penguin 2006.

Lintott, Andrew. *Violence in Republican Rome*, 2nd Edition, Oxford: Oxford University Press 1999.

Lovett, Frank. *A General Theory of Domination and Justice*, Oxford: Oxford University Press 2010.

MacCormack, Sabine. 'Cicero in Late Antiquity', in Catherine Steel (ed.), *Cambridge Companion to Cicero*, Cambridge: Cambridge University Press 2013.

Manuwald, Gesine. *Cicero*, London: I.B. Tauris 2015.

Marsh, David. 'Cicero in the Renaissance', in Catherine Steel (ed.), *The Cambridge Companion to Cicero*, Cambridge: Cambridge University Press 2013.

Maynor, John W. *Republicanism in the Modern World*, Cambridge: Polity 2003.

McCloskey, H. J. 'Rights – Some Conceptual Issues', *Australasian Journal of Philosophy*, Vol. 54, No. 2, August 1976.

Misak, Cheryl. *Pragmatism and Deliberation*, London: Routledge 2000.

Mitchell, Thomas. *Cicero the Senior Statesman*, New Haven, CT: Yale University Press 1991.

Moraes Santos, Igor. 'Montesquieu on Cicero. Historiographical, Political, and Philosophical Dimensions of a Modern Portrait', in Francesca Romana Berno and Giuseppe La Bua (eds.), *Portraying Cicero in Literature, Culture, and Politics: From Ancient to Modern Times*, Berlin: De Gruyter 2022.

Morello, Ruth. 'Further Voices and Familiar Perspectives in Cicero's Letters', *Hermathena*, No. 202–3, Summer-Winter 2017 (2022).

Nauert Jr., Charles. *Humanism and the Culture of Renaissance Europe*, 2nd Edition, Cambridge: Cambridge University Press 2006.

Nederman, Cary J. *The Bonds of Humanity: Cicero's Legacies in European Social and Political Thought, ca. 1100–ca. 1550*, University Park: Pennsylvania State University Press 2020.

Nelis, Jan. 'Constructing Fascist Identity: Benito Mussolini and the Myth of "Romanità"', *The Classical World*, Vol. 100, No. 4, Summer, 2007.

Nenci, Francesca. 'Introduzione', *Cicerone: La Repubblica*, Milan: Rizzoli 2008.

Nicgorski, Walter. *Cicero's Skepticism and His Recovery of Political Philosophy*, New York: Palgrave 2016.

Nozick, Robert. *Anarchy, State, Utopia*, Oxford: Blackwell 1974.

Nussbaum, Martha. 'Political Philosophy and International Feminism', in C. P. Ragland and S. Heidt (eds.), *What Is Philosophy?*, New Haven, CT: Yale University Press 2001.

O'Neill, Onora. *A Question of Trust: The BBC Reith Lectures 2002*, Cambridge: Cambridge University Press 2002.

O'Neill, Onora. 'The Dark Side of Human Rights', *International Affairs*, Vol. 81, No. 2, 2005.

Overall, Christine. 'How Old Is Old? Changing Conceptions of Old Age', in G. Scarre (ed.), *The Palgrave Handbook of the Philosophy of Aging*, London: Palgrave 2016.

Owen, David. *What Do We Owe to Refugees?*, Cambridge: Polity 2020.

Parekh, Serena. *No Refuge: Ethics and the Global Refugee Crisis*, Oxford: Oxford University Press 2020.

Parenti, Michael. *The Assassination of Julius Caesar: A People's History of Ancient Rome*, New York: The New Press 2003.

Petrarch. 'Old Grammarian', in J. H. Robertson (ed.), *Petrarch: The First Modern Scholar and Man of Letters*, London and New York: G.P. Putnam's Sons 1898.

Pettit, Philip. *Republicanism: A Theory of Freedom and Government*. Oxford: Oxford University Press 1997.

Philippe Rousellot, Philippe, 'Cicéron face aux dictateurs, 1920–1945', in Francesca Romana Berno and Giuseppe La Bua (eds.), *Portraying Cicero in Literature, Culture, and Politics: From Ancient to Modern Times*, Berlin: De Gruyter 2022.

Plutarch. *Fall of the Roman Republic, Six Lives*, translated by Rex Warner, London: Penguin Classics 1958.

Plutarch. 'The Life of Caius Gracchus', in *Lives*, Vol. X, Cambridge, MA: Harvard University Press 1989.

Przeworski, Adam. *Democracy and the Market: Political and Economic Reforms in Eastern Europe and Latin America*. Cambridge: Cambridge University Press 1991.

Quassim, Cassam. *Self-Knowledge for Humans*, Oxford: Oxford University Press 2015.

Rachman, Gideon. *The Age of the Strongman: How the Cult of the Leader Threatens Democracy around the World*, London: Vintage 2022.

Rama, José, Lisa Zanotti, Stuart J. Turnbull-Dugarte, Andrés Santana, *VOX: The Rise of the Spanish Populist Radical Right*, London: Routledge 2021.

Rawson, Elizabeth. *Cicero: A Portrait*, London: Allen Lane 1975.

Reinhold, Meyer. 'The Influence of Cicero on John Adams', *Ciceroniana on Line: A Journal of Roman Thought*, Vol. 8, 2015.

Remer, Gary. *Ethics and the Orator: The Ciceronian Tradition of Political Morality*, Chicago: University of Chicago Press 2017.

Rousseau, Jean-Jacques. *Reveries of the Solitary Walker*, Oxford: Oxford University Press 2011.

Ryan, Alan. *On Politics: A History of Political Thought from Herodotus to the Present*, London: Allen Lane 2012.

Schofield, Malcolm. *Cicero: Political Philosophy*, Oxford: Oxford University Press 2021.

Scullard, H. H. *From the Gracchi to Nero*, 5th Edition, London: Routledge 1982.

Shackleton Bailey, David. *Cicero*, London: Duckworth 1971.

Shklar, Judith. *The Faces of Injustice*. New Haven, CT: Yale University Press 1990.

Shklar, Judith. *On Political Obligation*, New Haven, CT: Yale University Press 2019.

Shotter, David. *The Fall of the Roman Republic*, London: Routledge 2005.

Stanley, Jason. *How Fascism Works: The Politics of Us and Them*, New York: Random House 2018.

Steel, Catherine. *Reading Cicero: Genre and Performance in Late Republican Rome*, London: Duckworth 2005.

Steiner, Hillel. *An Essay on Rights*, Oxford: Blackwell 1994.

Stothard, Peter. *Crassus: The First Tycoon*, New Haven, CT: Yale University Press 2022.

Takada, Y. 'Shakespeare's Cicero', in Mary Ann McGrail (ed.), *Shakespeare's Plutarch*, Special Issue of *Poetica: An International Journal of Linguistic-Literary Studies*, Vol. 48, Tokyo: Shubun International 1997.

Taylor, Lily Ross. *Party Politics in the Age of Caesar*, Berkeley: California University Press 1949.

Tempest, Katheryn. *Brutus: The Noble Conspirator*, New Haven, CT: Yale University Press 2017.

Tempest, Kathryn. *Cicero: Politics and Persuasion in Ancient Rome*, London: Bloomsbury 2011.

Tracy, Catherine. 'The People's Consul: The Significance of Cicero's Use of the Term "Popularis"', *Illinois Classical Studies*, No. 33–4, 2008–2009.

Treggiari, Susan. 'Consent to Marriage: Some Aspects of Law and Reality', *Echos du Monde Classique/Classical Views*, Vol. 26, No. 1, 1982.

Treggiari, Susan. *Terentia, Tullia and Publilia: The Women of Cicero's Family*, London: Routledge 2007.

Trollope, Anthony. *The Life of Cicero*, Vol. 2, London: The Trollope Society 1993.

Vasaly, Ann. 'The Political Impact of Cicero's Speeches', in Catherine Steel (ed.), *The Cambridge Companion to Cicero*, Cambridge: Cambridge University Press 2013.

Vergara, Camila. 'Populism as Plebeian Politics: Inequality, Domination, and Popular Empowerment', *The Journal of Political Philosophy*, Vol. 28, No. 2, 2020.

Vernon, Mark. *The Philosophy of Friendship*, Basingstoke: Palgrave 2005.

Viroli, Maurizio. *Republicanism*, New York: Hill and Wang 1999.

Vishnia, Rachel Feig. *Roman Elections in the Age of Cicero*, London: Routledge 2012.

Volk, Katharina. *The Roman Republic of Letters: Scholarship, Philosophy, and Politics in the Age of Cicero and Caesar*, Princeton: Princeton University Press 2021.

Whitten, Suzanne. *A Republican Theory of Free Speech: Critical Civility*, London: Palgrave 2021.

White, F. C. 'Love and Beauty in Plato's Symposium', *The Journal of Hellenic Studies*, Vol. 109, 1989.

Wilcox, Amanda. 'Cicero the Satirist? Scurrilous Poses in the Letters', *Hermathena*, Nos. 202–3, Summer-Winter 2017 (2022).

Wood, Neal. *Cicero's Social and Political Thought*, Berkeley, CA: University of California Press 1991.

Woolf, Raphael. *The Philosophy of a Roman Sceptic*, London: Routledge 2015.

Wyke, Maria (ed.), *Julius Caesar in Western Culture*, Malden, MA: Blackwell 2006.

Wyke, Maria. *Caesar in the USA*, Berkeley, CA: University of California Press 2012.

Yavetz, Zvi. 'Cicero: A Man of Letters in Politics', in Gillian Clark and Tessa Rajak (eds.), *Philosophy and Power in the Greco-Roman World*, Oxford: Oxford University Press.

Young, Iris Marion. *Justice and the Politics of Difference*, Princeton, NJ: Princeton University Press 1990.

Zetzel, James. 'Political Philosophy', in Catherine Steel (ed.), *Cambridge Companion to Cicero*, Cambridge: Cambridge University Press 2013.

Index